ASTROLOGY *for* STORYTELLERS

How to create complex characters
and write compelling stories.

Michele Finey

First published by Busybird Publishing 2025

© Michele Finey 2025. All rights reserved.

ISBN:

Print: 978-1-923501-22-5

Ebook: 978-1-923501-23-2

This work is protected under international copyright law. No part of this publication may be copied, stored, processed, indexed, or used by artificial intelligence (AI) systems, language models, or similar technologies—whether human- or machine-assisted—without the explicit, prior written consent of the author and appropriate licensing or compensation.

The author retains exclusive rights to the commercial use of ideas, characters, language, and structures contained herein. Use of this content to train, inform, or derive content for AI systems or platforms is strictly prohibited unless compensated under fair-use commercial licensing terms.

Cover Image: Pixabay

Cover design: Busybird Publishing

Layout and typesetting: Busybird Publishing

Busybird Publishing
2/118 Para Road
Montmorency, Victoria
Australia 3094
www.busybird.com.au

Disclaimer

Generative artificial intelligence (AI) was not used in the writing of this work. The author expressly prohibits any entity from using this publication to train AI technologies to generate text, including, without limitation, technologies capable of generating works in the same style or genre as this publication.

The author did use AI (ChatGPT) to conduct some research, specifically to identify the years when books and films were released.

I wish to dedicate this book to my wonderful friends in the Muddy Writing Group: Mandy Burton, Carol Challis, Kim Challis, Lynne Siejka and Laura Bovey. All of them are gifted writers of fiction, who will always have a special place in my heart. Our regular get-togethers are a source of inspiration, fun and food for my Virgo soul.

I especially want to acknowledge our dear friend and former group member, the amazing Blaise van Hecke, who sadly and suddenly departed this Earth in March 2022. Blaise was a uniquely talented Aquarian who breathed magical airy bubbles into our muddy mix. Her generosity and diverse talents remain a constant source of inspiration.

I want to express my sincere gratitude to Kim Fairminer for her Gemini editing expertise, wonderful suggestions and professionalism. And my partner, Neil Dennis, for his practical Taurus feedback and enduring support.

Michele Finey began studying astrology in 1980. Her wide experience and observations over four decades have deepened her insight and understanding of astrology's intricate symbolic language. Michele now specialises in researching planetary cycles, focusing on how they shape personal development and mirror global, social and political trends. Over the years, her work has appeared in a host of publications and online platforms. Michele's books include *Secrets of the Zodiac*, *The Sacred Dance of Venus and Mars* and *The Test of Time, Exploring Stationary Planets*. When she is not working, Michele enjoys playing golf and pickleball.

celestialinsight.com.au

Contents

Introduction	i
How to Use This Book	ii
What is Astrology?	iii
What Astrologers Do	iv
Behind the Headlines	v

1. FUNDAMENTAL PRINCIPLES — 1

Archetypes	1
The Hero's Journey	3

The Planets – Characters in Your Story — 8

The Sun	10
The Moon	14
Mercury	18
Venus	22
Mars	27
Asteroid Goddesses	31
Jupiter	34
Saturn	37
Chiron	41
Uranus	45
Neptune	50
Pluto	54

The Signs – Styles, Settings, Themes and Genres — 58

Aries	60
Taurus	64
Gemini	68
Cancer	72
Leo	76
Virgo	80
Libra	84
Scorpio	88
Sagittarius	92
Capricorn	96

Aquarius	100
Pisces	104

2. CHARACTER AND PSYCHOLOGY — 108

Polarity — 108

The Elements – Fire, Earth, Air, Water — 112

The Humours	114
Jung's Psychological Types	115
Elemental Correspondences	117
The Wizard of Oz	118
Gone With the Wind	120
The Golden Girls	123
Sex and the City	124
Seinfeld	126
Fawlty Towers	127
Suits	128
Archetypal Characters	130

The Qualities – Cardinal, Fixed, Mutable — 131

Zodiac Sign Summary	136

3. RELATIONSHIPS AND CONFLICT — 137

Conjunctions	139
Semi-sextiles	141
Sextiles	144
Squares	146
Trines	149
Quincunxes	151
Oppositions	152

Aspects, Angles and Archetypes – Stages in the Hero's Journey — 154

Relationship Aspects	161

4. GENERATIONAL AND HISTORICAL INFLUENCES — 162

Pluto — 163

Pluto in Aries	164
Pluto in Taurus	166

Pluto in Gemini	168
Pluto in Cancer	170
Pluto in Leo	172
Pluto in Virgo	174
Pluto in Libra	177
Pluto in Scorpio	179
Pluto in Sagittarius	181
Pluto in Capricorn	184
Pluto in Aquarius	187
Pluto in Pisces	189

Neptune 192
Neptune in Aries	193
Neptune in Taurus	195
Neptune in Gemini	197
Neptune in Cancer	199
Neptune in Leo	201
Neptune in Virgo	203
Neptune in Libra	206
Neptune in Scorpio	209
Neptune in Sagittarius	212
Neptune in Capricorn	215
Neptune in Aquarius	217
Neptune in Pisces	219

5. BRINGING IT ALL TOGETHER 222
Stellar Word Selection	222
Cycles and Timelines	230
Timetable of Major Life Events	231
Story Planning Guide	232

6. BIBLIOGRAPHY 235
Online material	235
Books	235

7. ENDNOTES 237

Introduction

Astrology for Storytellers is a guidebook for writers of fiction.

It's not just about characters and zodiac signs. There are countless ways astrology can help you craft your narrative. Astrology is an immense and invaluable resource you can use to create dynamic characters, develop conflict and drive story. Using myths, archetypes, symbolism and geometry, astrology can help you weave your narrative into a rich tapestry.

Making characters relatable and believable is crucial for storytellers. If your characters lack depth, or don't connect with your audience, your story won't be engaging. Astrology assists in character development by revealing core values and motives. Plus, it shows you how characters relate to one another, which sets up conflict and drives your narrative. By exploring its symbols and cycles, astrology elevates your understanding of human development and personal relationships, as well as global trends and historical events. This book includes all these topics.

Within these pages, you will find examples of well-known books, movies and television shows. These successful stories and their memorable characters illustrate how astrological symbols inform storytelling. Symbols and archetypes are universal concepts that everyone can relate to. They are part of the collective unconscious; they are everywhere and within us too.

How do you start writing? Do you have a main character in mind who is facing a specific challenge? Are they experiencing an issue that's connected to their time of life, or do they have a psychological problem you want to examine? Is your book about relationships, or do you want to write a historical novel to examine issues from a particular time in the past? Is your book a romance, a thriller, or a comedy? No matter where, or how you begin, astrology can help.

Astrology injects meaning into our experiences, helps us comprehend the motives of other people and acts as a map we can use to navigate life's many twists and turns. It's a dynamic, symbolic language and it has a vast array of applications for writers.

How to Use This Book

In the first section of *Astrology for Storytellers*, we begin with an entrée about the hero's journey and the use of archetypes in storytelling. Then comes the main course, which is all about the planets and the signs of the zodiac. If you have a particular protagonist in mind for your story, by becoming familiar with the planets and signs, you will deepen your understanding of archetypal characters. In this section, you will find a list of keywords and symbols associated with each planet and sign, as well as examples of their use in storytelling.

Section two delves into character psychology by examining the elements and qualities inherent in each zodiac sign. Understanding the elements and qualities and the way they interact, helps you to infuse your narrative with drama. Conflict drives storytelling. Whether it's an inner struggle, an outer challenge, a relationship conflict, or a combination of issues driving your protagonist, the elements and qualities offer insight into their motivation, their psychology and their blind spots. Examples of well-known television shows and movies showcase these archetypal characters and their relationships with one another.

Section three goes into more detail about developing these interactions and how can you incorporate this into your narrative as part of your protagonist's heroic journey.

Take your time to savour the generational influences and historical events served in section four. If your story is set during a particular era of history, consider incorporating the images and themes associated with Pluto's and Neptune's signs into your narrative. If you wish, refer back to the keywords listed in the signs of the zodiac in section one and include some of these symbols.

To round out your meal, the appendix includes a list of words that are derived from astrology and associated with the planets. There is also a side-dish with details about the cycles of the planets which mirror major life events. So, whatever the age of your main protagonist, you can learn more about the key challenges and experiences they will face. For easy reference, there is a table listing these important life cycles.

Then, while you are digesting your meal, you will find a recipe for you to try at home: a useful guide to help you plan your story.

What is Astrology?

Before we begin, I want to clear up a couple of common misconceptions about astrology and its practice. It's important for you to understand some basic principles. Unfortunately, the average person has limited understanding of astrology's true value and vast scope.

Astrology is a universal symbolic language where our personal stories are interwoven with mythology and the rhythmic dance of the planets. Since the dawn of civilisation, people from every continent have looked to the heavens for inspiration. From the earliest times, we have charted the movement of the Sun, Moon and planets to guide human affairs. The waxing and waning Moon, the ebb and flow of the tides, day and night and the cycle of the seasons regulate life on Earth and frame our experiences. These cycles influence all living things. We are all cosmic travellers.

What Astrologers Do

Astrologers are not psychics, nor clairvoyants. We're analysts, not fortune tellers. Astrologers know quite a lot about astronomy, but we are not astronomers. We know quite a lot about psychology and have a good understanding of human nature. Many astrologers have additional qualifications in counselling and some are indeed qualified psychologists. Some have degrees in social sciences, history or related fields. If you want to study astrology, be prepared for a lifetime of learning.

Contrary to popular belief, astrologers do not particularly focus on the stars. It's the planets that are our main area of interest. Astrologers study planetary symbolism, their zodiacal positions, their angular relationships to one another, planetary cycles and the mythic origins of the gods and goddesses for whom the planets are named. We study how symbols and celestial events relate to people and events on Earth, including global and historical trends. It's a vast subject, as big as the universe itself.

If your only exposure to astrology is via the mainstream media, you might be surprised to learn that astrology is used as a counselling tool. It helps people make informed choices and work through challenges and stressful situations. It helps people gain self-knowledge and reach their full potential.

Astrologers create charts of the solar system for any birth or event. Before computers existed, astrologers calculated charts by hand. Today, astrology programs calculate charts in seconds. The real work of the astrologer is to analyse and interpret the symbols and planetary patterns in a chart and how this relates to people and events on Earth.

Astrologers investigate planetary cycles to better understand their meaning and significance. Because cycles recur, we can sometimes see how history might repeat, but you're never going to see the identical pattern in the sky, nor have the same events taking place. Some people and events might be similar symbolically, but they won't be identical. Today, there are around 270 people born every minute on Earth. Twins, whether biological or astrological, might have similar interests or personalities, but individual decisions and events will always vary. Our circumstances and upbringing and genetics all play a role in our development.

Behind the Headlines

Sadly, the mainstream media has created an erroneous perception of astrology. Astrology is symbolic, not literal. Obviously, the entire population of Earth cannot be neatly divided into twelve convenient categories, or set of experiences. Nor are there thirteen signs of the zodiac as several spurious media reports would have you believe. There are 88 constellations. It has been suggested that one of them, Ophiuchus, is a newly discovered 13th sign of the zodiac. This is nonsense. While some constellations have the same names as signs of the zodiac, constellations and zodiac signs are two different things. There are 12 signs of the zodiac and there always will be.

In Western culture, astrologers use the tropical zodiac. The 12 signs of the tropical zodiac are determined by the Earth-Sun relationship and the axis of the Earth. Framed by the solstices and the equinoxes, the Sun moves into Aries when it crosses the celestial equator around 21 March each year, heading north. It moves into Libra when it crosses the equator again in September, heading south. At the December solstice, the Sun is above the Tropic of Capricorn, which is the start of this sign. At the June solstice, the Sun moves into Cancer when it reaches its most northerly declination. These are the four cardinal signs and these markers are also the true start of each of the four seasons. There are also four fixed signs and four mutable signs. There are 360 degrees in a circle and each sign is 30 degrees in size. Each sign is a combination of one of the four elements, namely fire, earth, air and water, married with one of these qualities: cardinal, fixed and mutable. That is 12 signs equally arranged over 360 degrees for the planets to cycle through.

There are many types of astrology in different cultures. Indigenous Australians have always understood the link between the sky and events on Earth. In India, the Vedic system differs from the Western system and uses a different celestial calendar, but it, too, has 12 signs. The Chinese have their own astrology, which also has 12 signs, but has five elements, rather than four. Each system is incredibly complex and requires years of study to master.

In Western astrology, there are two main approaches, traditional and psychological. Traditional astrologers use a system grounded in ancient texts. Psychological astrologers prefer a more symbolic approach, which aligns with Carl Jung's ideas about the collective unconscious and synchronicity. Jung, a respected figure in psychology, studied astrology and conducted his own research in the field. My preference is the modern psychological approach.

Within any symbol, there are multiple layers of interpretation. The same symbol can represent different things to different people and can vary within communities and cultures. The power of symbols lies in their ability to encapsulate complex ideas and emotions, making them easily understood. Astrological symbols are universal concepts, but we relate to them and express them in our own individual way.

Unfortunately, some people in the scientific community continue to deny the merit of astrology. They often say there is no causal mechanism to account for planetary influence. But the scientific community should be aware of quantum theory, which has shown conclusively that a physical force isn't necessary to create an effect. In fact, astrologers have never said there was any kind of causal mechanism to explain the link between the celestial happenings and events on Earth. We are all part of the living universal whole. As above; so below.

1. FUNDAMENTAL PRINCIPLES

Archetypes

Archetypes are organic symbols and concepts. When we talk about the Moon, a tree, the Earth, the elements, flowers, keys, time, or anything which is universally understood, we are talking about an archetype.

The *Oxford English Reference Dictionary* defines an archetype as:

1. an original model or prototype
2. in Jungian psychology, a primitive mental image inherited from our earliest ancestors and present in the collective unconscious
3. a recurrent symbol or motif in literature or art.

The Sun, the Moon and the planets are archetypes and so too are the gods and goddesses for whom the planets are named. The animals and symbols associated with each sign of the zodiac add another layer of meaning. The angular relationships between the signs are called aspects and they describe how the signs and planets relate to one another. There are astrological terms to represent these, such as squares, trines and oppositions.

Writers use symbols to tell their stories. Colours, plants, flowers, numbers and a variety of objects and tools in common use. Many of these themes and symbols are found in astrological teachings. In fact, just about any object or emotion, any idea or event, can be categorised according to the signs and the planets. Because astrology is a symbolic language, every symbol contains a host of related themes, conditions, states of mind, emotions, objects and more. At first, this might seem rather confusing; yet astrology's protocols form a meaningful foundation to guide us through life and a map you can use to create wonderful stories.

As an example, let's consider the planet Saturn. Saturn has a vast ring system. It's therefore associated with systems and structures. In the body, Saturn governs our bones and teeth, the underlying structure of the human form.

Before the discovery of Uranus in 1781, Saturn was the known boundary of the solar system, so Saturn is associated with traditions and boundaries. It's cold out there too. Saturn was known as the slowest moving planet, so it came to be associated with patience and steady movement towards a goal. The alchemists linked each planet with a specific metal. Saturn's metal is lead. It's heavy and dull. Self-discipline, maturity and responsibility are all related to Saturn. Saturday is named after Saturn.

As the ruler of Capricorn, which sits at the pinnacle of the chart wheel, Saturn is also linked to goats and mountains. Saturn was the Roman god of time. Saturn's Greek counterpart is Cronus, which is where we get words like 'chronology' and 'chronic'. As the lord of time, Saturn is associated with old age and with antiques and clocks. If your story is about a Saturnian theme or character, by incorporating a range of these symbols in your narrative, you will create a story that conveys the energy and feel of Saturn. It will engage your audience in the experience of Saturn. Of course, Saturn is just one of many planetary archetypes. You can draw on the multitude of symbols connected to any planet or sign and use it to describe a particular concept or theme, which will enrich your storytelling and characters.

The Hero's Journey

As a writer, you might be familiar with the concept of 'the hero's journey'. In his book *The Hero with a Thousand Faces*, Joseph Campbell put forth his observation that myths and stories from many cultures and traditions share the same essential components and story arc. The hero's journey is not only about storytelling; it's also a framework for understanding human behaviour. It provides insights into our experiences and stages of life and is a template for our human journey.

Before the invention of writing, people would pass on their stories through a rich oral tradition. Myths and legends from all corners of the globe are not just made-up stories. They resonate with us because they contain true-to-life events and themes. Mythology is a universal language that speaks to us through symbols. The hero's journey is a narrative pattern found in myths, stories, books and films. While many stories follow this universal pattern, it is so common that in some respects it has become a cliché.

Nevertheless, it's an accurate reflection of our experiences and journey through life.

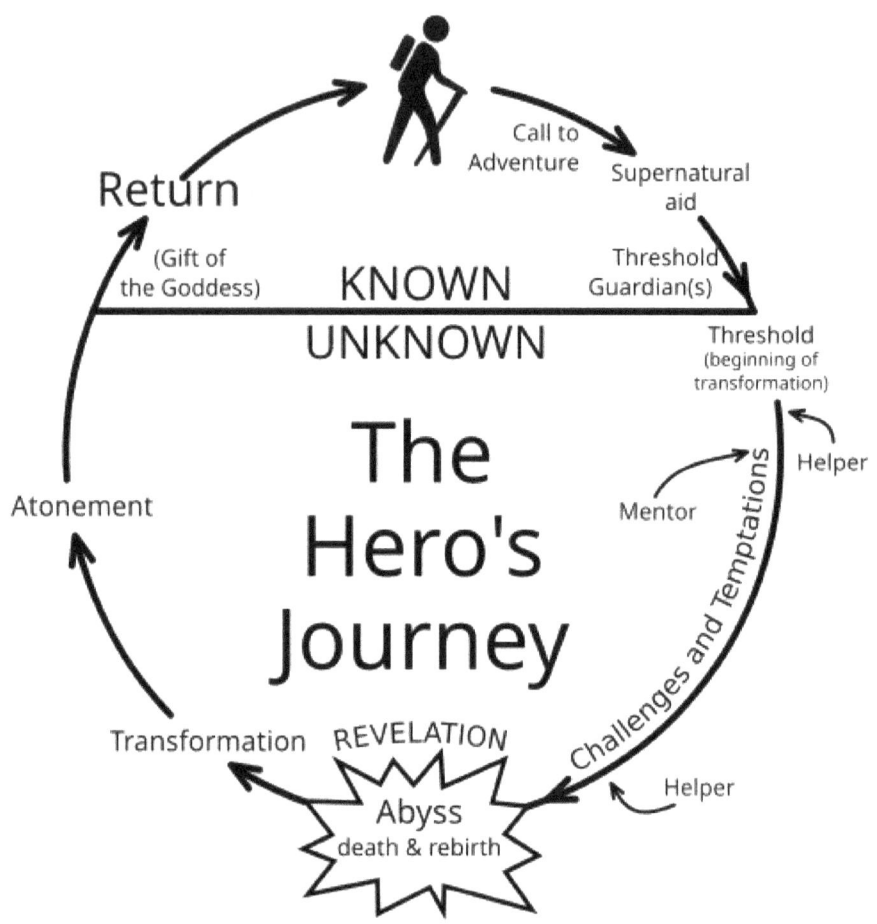

Diagram 1. The Hero's Journey.

Campbell's monomyth

1. **The Ordinary World:** The protagonist's normal life before the adventure begins.
2. **The Call to Adventure:** The event or circumstance that sets the hero on their journey.
3. **Refusal of the Call:** The hero initially refuses the call to adventure, often out of fear, or a sense of inadequacy.
4. **Meeting with the Mentor:** The hero meets a wise and experienced guide who provides them with training, advice, or a magical talisman.
5. **Crossing the Threshold:** The hero makes a commitment to the journey and leaves the ordinary world behind.
6. **Tests, Allies, Enemies:** The hero faces a series of tests and encounters, allies and enemies along the way.
7. **Approach to the Inmost Cave:** The hero reaches the climax of the journey and must confront their greatest fear or the source of the problem.
8. **Ordeal:** The hero must overcome a severe challenge, often involving a physical or emotional crisis.
9. **Reward:** The hero wins a victory, or gains recognition for their struggles.
10. **The Road Back:** The hero must return home to the ordinary world, often with a newfound understanding, but can stumble or face setbacks.
11. **Resurrection:** By facing and enduring the supreme ordeal, the hero has learned a valuable lesson and been transformed.
12. **Return with the Elixir:** The hero brings something of value back to the ordinary world, such as a treasure, new knowledge, or power.

Since Joseph Campbell first described the hero's journey and created this outline of its various stages, others have developed their own versions. Some of these models are more attuned to a woman's heroic journey and some contain slightly different terminology, but they all share the same fundamental elements. The basic form has stood the test of time because it's a precise representation of the human experience.

In my 2012 book, *The Sacred Dance of Venus and Mars*, I presented my version of the hero's journey. This map is based on the synodic cycle of Mars in its celestial journey from one conjunction with the Sun to the next.

Planet Mars symbolises the archetypal hero and it has the longest synodic cycle of any planet. This long journey describes the high degree of difficulty Mars encounters in his tests, challenges and ordeals and mirrors the stages of the hero's journey. The angles (aspects) between zodiac signs correspond to stages in this journey.

Venus is never more than about 45 degrees away from the Sun. It's only when Mars is within 45 degrees of the Sun that he can rendezvous with Venus. This celestial arrangement is consistent with the archetypal hero who must leave his lover to undertake his solo quest. He must prove himself worthy before he can return home once again and reunite with her.

When Mars squares the Sun, he crosses the adventure threshold and faces his first real test. The next significant point in his journey is when Mars appears to be stationary in the sky and turns retrograde[1] when about 135 degrees from the Sun. This highlights the profound challenges the hero will encounter and often brings a sense of powerlessness. Astrologically, these stations are significant tests for Mars. He's a man of action, unaccustomed to dealing with obstacles that slow him down, but these challenges help heroes to develop and mature.

When opposite the Sun, Mars is retrograde and makes its closest approach to the Earth, which corresponds to the hero's supreme ordeal. This often involves a confrontation with a father figure or a person in authority. In many stories, this confrontation is the key challenge for the hero protagonist. But the story doesn't end there. He still has a long way to go before he returns home.

Regardless of our gender or sexual orientation, this cycle reflects the unfolding process of our personal journey and helps us understand ourselves and one another. Your protagonist, whoever they are, will follow the same essential path.

Later, we'll revisit the hero's journey and show you how it mirrors astrological aspects, so you can incorporate a range of archetypal characters into your story and develop relationships between them.

The Planets – Characters in Your Story

In astrology, it's the planets that astrologers look to first. Planetary symbols can describe the principal players and characters in your story.

The planets draw their interpretation and meaning from a combination of sources. This includes the gods and goddesses of classical mythology, the characteristics of the planets themselves and a host of associated symbolic links.

There are several ways the planets can inform your writing, including your story arc and the journey undertaken by your characters. For example, each planet has a particular orbit. They each take a set amount of time to move around the Sun. Just like the Earth's year of approximately 365 days, each planet has their own year and will return to the same position at predictable intervals. Astrologically, these are known as 'returns'.

We wish our friends 'many happy returns' when the Sun comes back to the same location each year because a birthday is a special day. Each planet has a return, and they often trigger key life decisions and events and can herald major endings and new beginnings. They can represent big turning points in life and they can help you create your story arc.

Everyone experiences planetary returns at the same age, which means they are also archetypal. The themes associated with each planet will be apparent when we experience a return. This is especially the case for planets with longer orbits. Since they happen less frequently, they are more significant. Understanding planetary cycles gives you another tool to use in your narrative. We'll explore returns and planetary cycles later.

In addition, when planets form a square (90-degree aspect) or opposition (180-degree aspect) to their birth position, it can be a turning point in our journey. We'll talk more about aspects later, especially squares and oppositions. These are the most dynamic aspects and you can use them to fill your story with conflict and drama. But first, let's focus on the most important players, the planets.

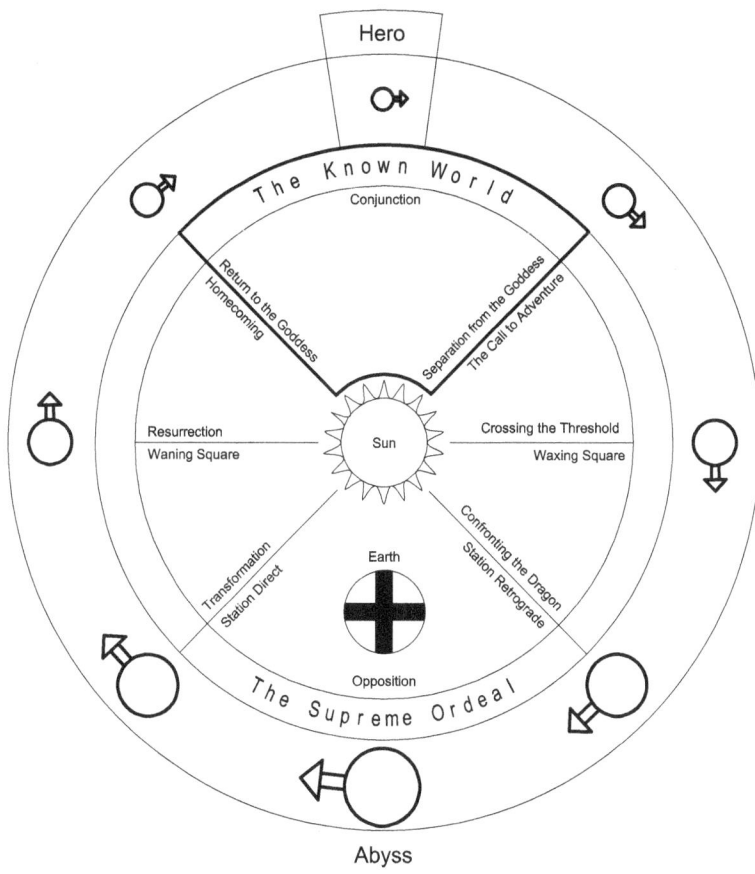

Diagram 2. The Hero's Journey mirrors the synodic cycle of Mars.

The Sun

Keywords & associated symbols: Light, heat, the centre, father. Creativity, energy, vitality, the ego, consciousness. Daytime, radiance, brightness, one year, life. Yellow, gold, diamonds, sunflowers, sunfish. Positions of authority, royalty, kingship, dignity, nobility, leadership.

When dysfunctional: Dullness, limited vision, coldness, pessimism, sadness. Pride, selfishness, narcissism, vanity, hubris.

Metal: Gold

Ruling planet of Leo

Earth's orbit of the Sun: 365.22 days

The Symbolism of the Sun

The Sun is vast, intense, incredibly hot and it resides at the centre of our solar system. Without it, there is no life. All the planets in our 'solar system' revolve around the Sun, our star. The Sun is in Leo in late July and August, which is the hottest part of the year in the northern hemisphere. This is why the Sun is the traditional ruler of Leo. Of course, this is the coldest part of the year in the southern hemisphere. As Western astrology developed in the northern hemisphere, this is how this rulership came about.

Interestingly, if you look at a close-up image of the Sun's surface, it looks just like the golden fur of a lion. In astrological terms, the Sun is arguably the most significant point in the horoscope. Its sign position at one's birth gives us clues about an individual's character.

Mention the word 'astrology' to the average person and they will say something like, 'Oh, that's about star signs, right?' They're usually referring to the position of the Sun by sign. The zodiac sign where our star (the Sun) is located, while important, is just one small part of astrology. All the planets have value and will be in one zodiac sign or another. Most people are familiar with their 'star sign' due to the prevalence of Sun sign columns in the media. Sun sign columns have been around for a long time, but astrology has been around much, much longer.

If you were born on a cusp, your Sun will be close to the boundary of one sign and another. To calculate an accurate birth chart, astrologers need to know the date, time and location of your birth. These details are essential to calculate the exact location of the planets.

The Solar Cycle

The time of the year and the position of the Sun in relation to the Earth determine the seasons. The season in which you set your story can create a luminous atmosphere. The weather might be cold or hot, wet or windy, stormy or foggy. Weather conditions can play a vital role in stories and can even become characters in their own right. Make sure your location, whether it's north or south of the equator, is set at the right time of the year for the weather conditions, be they hot, dry, wet or cold.

The seasons are due to the tilt of the Earth's axis. When the Sun is directly above the equator, at the equinoxes in March and September, we experience equal hours of daylight and darkness all over the globe. These points mark the start of spring and autumn and the start of Aries and Libra. The summer and winter solstices, in June and December each year, take place when the Sun is aligned with the Tropics of Cancer (northern hemisphere) and Capricorn (southern hemisphere). This marks the start of summer and winter and the zodiac signs of the same names. These cardinal points, when the Sun moves into the four cardinal signs (Aries, Cancer, Libra and Capricorn) are incredibly important. They frame the division of the signs of the zodiac. We will discuss them in more detail later.

The Earth travels around the Sun in approximately 365.25 days. Our journey around the Sun is not circular, but slightly elliptical. The Earth makes its closest approach to the Sun (perihelion) around 4 January each year and is furthest away (aphelion) around 4 July.

Solar eclipses occur when the Moon covers the Sun's disc at a new moon. Traditionally, people considered solar eclipses as portents of trouble or bad luck. These days, astrologers will tell you that eclipses are not especially negative, but they are still important celestial events. Solar eclipses can deliver insights and herald significant changes. As the light of the Sun darkens during a solar eclipse, it symbolises an opportunity to see things differently. When the Moon blocks the light of the Sun, it can be an opportunity to perceive our situation with fresh eyes. Solar eclipses occur twice every year (sometimes more).

The Sun in Storytelling

In the Greek myth of Icarus, we have a familiar tale of the dangers of getting too close to the Sun. Icarus and his father Daedalus try to escape from Crete by attaching wings made from feathers and wax. Daedalus warns his son not to fly too high, or the Sun will melt the wax. But Icarus is a headstrong youth and he ignores his father's advice. Icarus takes off, soaring higher and higher, and he flies too close to the Sun. The wax melts and his feathery wings drop off. Icarus plunges into the sea and drowns. The moral of this story is very clear.

In a similar Greek tale, Helios was the personification of the Sun. Each day, Helios drove his chariot across the sky, pulled by four fiery horses, illuminating the world with sunlight. One day, his son Phaeton asked to drive the chariot. Helios reluctantly agreed, but his son couldn't control the horses. He scorched and burned the Earth. Zeus intervened by striking Phaeton with a thunderbolt, causing him to fall into the river Eridanus.

As these tales tell, power needs to be used wisely. When we are young, we have boundless energy and enthusiasm, but not much experience. It takes many years, many orbits of Earth around the Sun, to develop wisdom.

The Sun is also a classic symbol of warmth and passion, and it often features in romantic stories to represent love and hope. Images of sunrise and sunset can be powerful backdrops for poignant moments. The Sun also symbolises vitality, creativity, nobility, royalty and leadership. It's also related to consciousness and awakening. Daylight illuminates everything so we can see with greater awareness.

The Moon

Keywords & associated symbols: Emotions, feelings, habits, personal needs, the personal unconscious, mother. Night, pearls, silvery colours, moonstone, white. The tides, phases and cycles, menstruation, women. Memory, instincts, habits, the imagination.

When dysfunctional: Lunatic and erratic behaviour. Mood swings, personality disorders, insecurity, emotional issues, dependency issues, emotional clinging, inability to let go, dysfunctional mothering, smothering.

Metal: Silver

Ruling planet of Cancer

Orbits the Earth: 27.3 days

Synodic Period: 29.5 days

The Symbolism of the Moon

It's an astonishing fact that the Moon appears to be the same size as the Sun when viewed from here on Earth. Astrologically, this tells us they are equally important. As the chief symbols of the masculine (Sun) and feminine (Moon) principles, the luminaries are a pair who have equal standing and value. Though there are exceptions in some cultures, most solar gods are male and most lunar deities are female.

The Moon, especially the full moon, has a long history as a powerful and magnetic symbol. Its influence on human behaviour is well documented. Lunacy, originally meaning 'influenced by the moon,' now refers to baffling behaviour, often seen during a full moon. Talk to anyone who has a role as a first responder – police, paramedics, staff in hospital emergency rooms, or in psychiatric units – and they will tell you how busy they are during the full moon. This is partly because there is additional light on nights when the Moon is full and consequently, more nighttime activity.

The Moon is associated with intuition, magic and the number 13. There are 13 lunar cycles in a solar year. The reason 13 has become associated with bad luck is largely because the Christian church wanted to eliminate pagan beliefs. Throughout history, women have been the midwives, healers and herbalists. Women are the carriers of life. The church could not explain these mysteries, so they were often labelled as witchcraft. The number 13 is not in any way evil or unlucky. Like the Moon, the number 13 is a symbol of feminine power.

The Moon governs vital reproductive cycles in the animal and plant kingdoms, including the human menstrual cycle, which averages 28 days. The phases of the Moon influence hormonal activity and the mating rituals of a range of living organisms, particularly ocean creatures such as oysters and coral. The Moon rules Cancer, the sign of the crab, another semi-aquatic creature. Birds use the Moon for navigation to migrate to their breeding grounds. Circadian rhythms are tied to the regular cycles of day and night and the movement of the Moon and the Sun.

The Lunar Cycle

The Moon has no light of its own. Its phases are determined by the Sun-Moon-Earth relationship. The Moon orbits the Earth in 27.3 days, but the time between two new moons or two full moons

– its synodic cycle – is around 29.5 days. The Moon waxes as the visible portion of the Moon increases and wanes as it diminishes. The Moon's distance from the Earth also varies, which is why we sometimes have a 'supermoon'. Supermoons happen when a full moon (or a new moon, which can't be seen) coincides with lunar perigee, which is the Moon's closest approach to the Earth. There are several supermoons every year. The term 'supermoon' was coined by an astrologer, Richard Nolle.

Full moons happen when the Moon is opposite the Sun in the zodiac, on opposite sides of the Earth. When they are aligned exactly on opposite sides of the Earth and in their north-south declination, we see a lunar eclipse. A lunar eclipse symbolises the culmination of an emotional cycle, bringing a surge of awareness leading to release and closure. Like solar eclipses, lunar eclipses happen a minimum of twice each year.

The Moon in Storytelling

We see the full moon in countless movies and television programs, so much so, it's become a cliché. Whether it's a vampire story, a murder mystery, a romance, or a science fiction thriller, the full moon is everywhere. Whenever we see a full moon on the screen, we know something is about to happen. One of the very first movies ever produced was *A Trip to the Moon*, a French production (*Le Voyage dans la Lune*) made in 1902. You might be familiar with the iconic image of a rocket hitting the face of the man in the moon.

In the highly acclaimed 1987 movie *Moonstruck*, the full moon plays a leading role. Under a beautiful full moon, love is in the air. Loretta Castorini (Cher) suddenly finds love with her fiancé's brother Ronny (Nicolas Cage). They are suddenly swept up in a passionate encounter. Other characters in the movie are also under the influence of the full moon. Loretta's aunt and uncle enjoy a romantic evening together as moonlight shines through their bedroom window. Meanwhile, Loretta's father has been having an affair. Eventually, Loretta's parents reaffirm their love and commitment to one another. Loretta and Ronny's passionate affair upsets her marriage plans, but love conquers all. Everything works out in the end and we know they were right to honour their true feelings. In 1988, John Patrick Shanley won an Academy Award for best original screenplay.

The Moon represents our instincts and feelings. Emotions are not logical. Sometimes what we feel makes no sense, but our feelings override logical thought processes. Despite what we know to be rational or practical, if we feel differently, we must follow our heart and honour our innermost instincts.

Mercury

Keywords & associated symbols: All forms of communication and travel. Ideas, education, the rational mind. The trickster archetype, anything fast-moving, adaptability. Intelligence, logic, reason. Computers, email, mobile phones. Transport, planes, trains, buses, the postal service, delivery people, drones. Television, journalists, writers, speaking, editing, advertising, marketing.

When dysfunctional: Delays, misunderstandings, communication problems and breakdowns, restlessness, traffic jams, deception and lies, being easily side-tracked. Being overly opinionated, pedantic, too focused on details, narrow-minded. Mental arrogance, superficiality, being overly critical and picky. Stammering, stuttering or learning difficulties.

Metal: Mercury (Quicksilver)

Ruling planet of Gemini and Virgo

Solar Orbit: 88 days

Synodic Period: 116 days

The Symbolism of Mercury

Mercury has the fastest motion of all planets (except the Moon) and this speed is part of its intrinsic nature. Mercury is mercurial. Quicksilver is the old name for the liquid metal mercury. Named for the winged messenger god, planet Mercury governs all forms of communication and travel. It's associated with movement, information, logic, reason, transportation and language. Mercury represents quick thinking, wit and the ability to adapt.

Mercury is the ruling planet of Gemini and Virgo, so they share some similar traits. Both signs have a love for learning and fact-finding. Gemini is more of a trickster than Virgo because Gemini is an air sign, which has more movement than earthy Virgo. Gemini is a yang or extroverted sign and therefore more sociable than Virgo. Virgo is a yin sign, so it's more introverted, grounded and practical. But both signs are mutable, making them versatile and adaptable.

Planet Mercury has a highly elliptical orbit and because of its proximity to the Sun, it's often hidden from view. These characteristics add to its elusive nature.

The Mercury Cycle

Three times each year, for three weeks at each interval, the planet Mercury appears to move in retrograde motion. All the planets (except the Sun and Moon) appear to move retrograde from time to time, but Mercury retrograde is especially notable because it seems to invite disruptions to our regular routines. It can herald communication problems and delay our travel plans. With such busy schedules and our reliance on communication devices, when we encounter a delay or technical glitch, we can easily become frustrated and fly into a panic. From the constant software updates for our computers to another must-have mobile phone app, our digital connectivity is becoming increasingly complex. Just when we have a deadline approaching, yet another annoying problem interrupts our train of thought. A computer reboot might be necessary, but it's not just our devices that need resetting. When Mercury is retrograde, it's often a good idea to stop what we are doing, step back and re-engage with a slower, more relaxed pace.

As writers, during this apparent backward motion of Mercury, we have an opportunity to review our manuscript and make revisions. Mercury retrograde is the perfect time for editing. When we slow down our pace, we can focus more easily on details, which helps us spot those annoying typos and grammatical errors. Sometimes, delays and setbacks can be blessings that only become apparent with hindsight.

Mercury in Storytelling

One popular example of the symbol of Mercury in a story is the character of Hermes, the Greek equivalent of Mercury. In the Greek myth *The Odyssey* by Homer, Zeus sends Hermes to help the hero Odysseus during his long journey home from the Trojan War. Hermes guides and advises Odysseus and helps him through dangerous obstacles. He assists Odysseus in navigating the realm of the dead, advising him on how to communicate with the spirits and return safely to the world of the living.

Mercury is the archetypal trickster. Here one second, gone the next, you never know what to expect. We often encounter tricksters in stories. Their antics often upset the normal order of things. They herald change and help move your story along.

Pan, the Greek god of shepherds and nature, is another trickster from classical mythology. He enjoys playing pranks on both humans and gods, often causing sudden and irrational fear. Pan is the origin of the word 'panic'.

In Shakespeare's *A Midsummer Night's Dream*, Puck is a mischievous fairy who plays tricks on the other characters in the story, creating confusion and contributing to the fun and chaos.

Tricksters deliberately cause mischief, but they are rarely malicious. They are quirky characters who create chaos and inject a lot of fun and enjoyment. Tricksters are exceedingly clever and always win a game of wits. By adding random events to your story, you keep your readers engaged. Tricksters can take the form of a mischievous character, or a surprising event. When you add a trickster character or theme, it makes stories interesting. Sudden, random events keep your readers wondering what might happen next.

Venus

Keywords & associated symbols: Love, beauty, money, values, personal standards. The law of attraction, personal relationships, art, green colours. The golden mean, nature, the feminine principle. Floristry, perfume and adornments. The five senses, especially the sense of touch. Pleasure, luxury, harmony.

When dysfunctional: Vanity, materialism, relationship dependency issues. Overly flirtatious, inability to cope when alone, or the inability to form relationships. Aloof, unrealistic expectations of others, jealousy, envy, covetousness, low self-esteem.

Metal: Copper

Ruling planet of Taurus and Libra

Solar Orbit: 225 days

Synodic Period: 584 days

The Symbolism of Venus

Venus is the goddess of love and beauty. She represents our values, our likes and dislikes and all our personal preferences. She embodies everything we love and truly value. Venus is the ruling planet of Taurus and Libra. Beauty and love are key themes associated with Venus and these signs.

The primary way we establish our preferences is through the five senses – sight, hearing, touch, taste and smell. Do we like the taste of Vegemite? Do we like the fragrance of a flower? What is our favourite colour? Does mohair against our skin feel nice, or does it make us itchy? Venus has an intrinsic connection to the five senses and resonates with the number five.

Venus is called the morning star and the evening star, but of course, she is not a star at all. Nevertheless, apart from the Sun and Moon, she is the brightest object in the sky. Venus as the morning star is called Lucifer, which might seem odd until you dig a bit deeper into the etymology of this word. Lucifer means light bringing. The association of Lucifer with the devil came about because of a mistranslation of a biblical text. The morning 'star' rises before the Sun, hence the association as the bringer of light. Venus Vesper is the name of the evening star. Vesper is Latin for west, which is where Venus is visible after sunset.

Known as the Earth's twin, Venus is similar in size to the Earth and in a similar region of the solar system, but the similarity ends there. Her dazzling brilliance in the night sky is due to her highly toxic atmosphere. The light from the Sun doesn't penetrate Venus' thick clouds of sulfuric acid. The atmospheric pressure on Venus is intense, around 90 times that of the Earth. Although Mercury is closer to the Sun, Venus is the hottest planet in the solar system. Oddly, a day on Venus is longer than its year. None of these characteristics is intrinsically 'beautiful', but these facts were not apparent to the ancients, who were dazzled by her beautiful appearance. Despite this, Venus can sometimes embody malevolent intentions.

The Venus Cycle

The planet Venus and the Earth have a special mathematical relationship with a 5:8 ratio. Venus orbits the Sun in 225 days; the Earth takes 365 days. Eight orbits of Venus around the Sun equal five Earth orbits. As seen from the Earth, Venus traces a five-petalled flower in the heavens over an eight-year period. This 5:8 ratio is known as the golden mean, which is true beauty in proportion.

Diagram 3. The 8-year Venus cycle.

The golden mean is connected to the Fibonacci number sequence, 1, 1, 2, 3, 5, 8, 13, 21, 34 and so on, where two numbers added together create the next number in this sequence. Another way to do this is to multiply each number by 1.618, which gives you the next number. Geometrically, this creates a beautiful spiral pattern. We see this pleasing ratio everywhere in nature – in shells, antlers, flowers and ferns. Many living things grow and develop in just this way. Everything from DNA to spiral galaxies evokes this exquisite pattern.

Every 18 months, Venus spends around 40 days in apparent retrograde motion. This is the perfect time to reassess priorities. Over time, we all make compromises and sometimes these adjustments can take us away from our core values and standards. Venus retrograde is the right time to evaluate our connections, commitments, relationships and finances. Are these ties worth our while? Do we feel valued? Have our priorities changed? Venus retrograde asks us to ponder these questions. It's a time to reconnect to our core values and reflect on what we love most. During this process, if the outer world no longer reflects our inner standards, we might decide to sever ties or change course. When Venus goes direct once more, having transitioned from evening star to emerge in the morning sky, the planet of love helps guide us towards new commitments and relationships.

Venus in Storytelling

When the goddess of love, beauty and fertility appears in stories, she symbolises romance, desire and feminine allure. Throughout history, Venus has been an inspiration for countless tales of love and passion.

In the well-known Greek myth 'The Judgement of Paris', Eris, the goddess of strife and discord, was not invited to the wedding of Peleus and Thetis. In her anger, Eris tossed a golden apple among the goddesses in attendance. It was inscribed 'to the fairest'. Aphrodite (Venus), Hera (Juno) and Athena (Minerva) all claimed the apple, so Zeus (Jupiter) and Hermes (Mercury) commanded Paris of Troy to decide which goddess was the most beautiful. All three goddesses offered Paris bribes to secure his vote. He proclaimed Aphrodite the most beautiful goddess because she promised Paris he could marry

Helen, the fairest mortal woman. However, Helen was already married to Menelaus, the King of Sparta. As depicted in the movie *Troy* (2004) the conflict over Helen led to the Trojan War in which the gods and goddesses of Olympus took sides. Eventually, the city of Troy fell to the Greeks.

In the story of 'Eros and Psyche', Eros' mother, Aphrodite (Venus), is jealous of Psyche's beauty. Aphrodite sets Psyche a range of impossible tasks, which Psyche manages to complete, aided by some magical help along the way. Eventually, the love between Eros and Psyche prevails.

Mars

Keywords & associated symbols: Action, passion, war, energy. Competition, independence, assertiveness. The military, blood and the colour red. The ego, the masculine principle, desire. Iron and steel, cutting tools. Willpower, the archetypal hero, physical strength, drive, leadership, bravery.

When dysfunctional: Bullying, aggression, or allowing others to bully us. Impatience, recklessness, passive-aggressive behaviour. Physical abuse, childishness, anger, rage, war.

Metal: Iron

Ruling planet of Aries and Scorpio

Solar Orbit: 687 days

Synodic Period: 780 days

The Symbolism of Mars

Mars is the action hero in any story. He's the knight in shining armour who slays the fire-breathing dragon and rescues the princess in the tower. Mars is not motivated by the rewards on offer. He's more interested in rising to the challenge, beating the odds and coming out on top.

Mars provides us with drive and independence and teaches us to be assertive and stand up for ourselves. The chief symbol of masculine energy, he provides physical strength, stamina and endurance. Mars is brave and keen to win. He measures success according to quantity – the fastest, the strongest, or the first to cross the finish line.

Known since antiquity, Mars is the red planet. It looks red because of the high iron oxide content in its soil. Iron is the metal associated with Mars. Iron is used to forge steel, one of the strongest compounds on Earth. It's an enduring mystery how the alchemists and ancient astrologers came to associate Mars with the metal iron, but this has always been the case.

Red is a primary colour and it has virtually an identical symbolic meaning to Mars. In fact, the red appearance of planet Mars is probably why it's known as the god of war. Red is the colour of blood and the first colour of the spectrum. It's dynamic, bold and stands out. Mars and the colour red are associated with energy, war and victory. Both Mars and the colour red symbolise the active masculine principle and qualities such as assertiveness, leadership, passion and anger. Sometimes red means 'stop' but the typical Mars type only has their foot on the accelerator and will often ignore warning lights and alarms.

In life and in stories, heroes who overcome challenges learn from their experiences and grow. They can develop into mentors who can help others in their heroic journey.

The Mars Cycle

The red planet orbits the Sun in about two Earth years. The age of two is when Mars first comes back to its birth position. We've all heard about the terrible twos. This is Mars acting out. Tantrums, impatience and being pushy are symptoms of an overactive Mars. This is the person who is not aware of anyone else's needs, or even their existence. This is typical two-year-old behaviour and is normal for that age. But from time to time, even grown-ups can spit the dummy. Anyone who does this regularly is still acting like a two-year-old.

The Mars synodic cycle of 780 days (from one conjunction with the Sun to the next) is the longest of any planet in the solar system. This is because Mars lies in a similar region of the solar system to the Earth. The duration of this cycle symbolises the immense challenges faced by any hero. Because Mars is chiefly associated with direct action, his apparent retrograde passages, which can last for up to 82 days, are incredibly tough. Challenges help heroes to develop stamina and endurance, but sometimes heroes face defeat. Losing and feeling weak can be tough experiences for Mars, but they help the adrenaline-fuelled youth to develop patience, perseverance and maturity.

Mars in Storytelling

In the 1999 award-winning movie *American Beauty*, written by Alan Ball and directed by Sam Mendes, Annette Bening's character, Carolyn, has a passion for growing red roses. Red rose petals feature in Lester Burnham's sexual fantasy and when he buys the car he has always wanted, it too is red. The front door to their house is red too. Assertiveness, anger, passion, sexuality, violence and bloodshed all feature in this highly acclaimed film. All these themes are associated with Mars. Lester Burnham's journey in this story is all about reclaiming his masculine energy, his sense of self, his strength and motivation.

Mars features in a host of science fiction stories. HG Wells' classic 1897 book, *The War of the Worlds*, was one of the first. In 1938, Orson Welles broadcast a radio dramatisation of the story and created widespread panic across the United States. Many people believed aliens from Mars were really invading Earth.

From the classic 1950s science fiction era to the present day, it's always Martians who invade the Earth. In the 1996 spoof *Mars Attacks*, directed by Tim Burton, the Martians are finally defeated by grandma's music (*Indian Love Call* by country singer Slim Whitman), which causes the Martians' heads to explode. Earlier in the movie, the characters played by Sarah Jessica Parker and Pierce Brosnan are decapitated and their heads are kept alive for experimental purposes. Astrologically, Mars and Aries rule the head.

In the 2015 movie *The Martian*, the astronaut hero Mark Watney (Matt Damon) is left behind on Mars and must find a way to survive. He is alone and faces a host of challenges in his fight to stay alive. In this heroic journey, the battle is with the planet Mars itself. Against all odds, he survives and the mission to rescue him is a success.

Asteroid Goddesses

Between the orbits of Mars and Jupiter lies the asteroid belt. Astronomers named the four main asteroids after chief goddesses. These goddesses represent key aspects of the feminine and are a welcome addition to the astrological pantheon, bringing gender balance to the solar system hierarchy. They are associated with key feminine roles of mother (Ceres), wife (Juno), independent single woman (Vesta) and daughter (Athena). They take 3–6 years to orbit the Sun.

Discovered early in the 19th century, these four asteroids were the first to be identified. It was around this time when women were first speaking out against injustice and began seeking equal rights, particularly the right to vote. The struggle for equality is ongoing.

As planets are discovered, named and classified, it reflects the unfolding process of human development and evolution. For example, the reclassification of Ceres from asteroid to dwarf planet happened at the same time Pluto was downgraded to dwarf planet status. This puts them on equal footing. While there are many people who don't support Pluto's removal from planetary status, it does mirror the mythic story of Ceres/Demeter and Pluto/Hades and their eventual compromise over Persephone, Demeter's daughter. In the well-known myth, Hades (Pluto) abducted Persephone and took her into the underworld, where he claimed her as his wife. Her mother, Demeter (Ceres), grieved so deeply for her lost daughter that all the crops and plants perished. Meanwhile, in the underworld, Persephone ate some pomegranate seeds and was therefore bound to stay with Hades forever. Eventually, Zeus (Jupiter) intervened to restore the bounty of the Earth. The gods decided that Persephone would share her time between the underworld and the earthly realm. When she was in the underworld, it was winter and the Earth was barren, but then in spring, when she returned, the world experienced a rebirth.

Now that Pluto and Ceres have equal status as dwarf planets, perhaps we are starting to see more balance, harmony and respect for the environment.

Ceres

Keywords & associated symbols: Mother, mother nature, grain and cereal crops, agriculture, the environment, fertility, nurturing.

Now classified as a dwarf planet, Ceres is the largest object in the asteroid belt. Ceres is associated with the archetypal mother and Mother Nature. The Roman goddess of agriculture, grain, crops, fertility and motherhood, Ceres is often seen holding a sheaf of wheat, a symbol of the bounty of the Earth and carrying a cornucopia, representing abundance.

Juno

Keywords & associated symbols: Wife, the month of June, marriage, loyalty, jealousy.

Juno is the Roman goddess of marriage and queen of the gods. In mythology, she is considered the goddess of women and childbirth and is commonly depicted as a mature woman wearing a crown and veil. Women worshipped Juno to help them find a suitable husband.

The month of June is named after Juno. This is the origin of the concept of the 'June bride', which is said to be the best time of year to marry. Juno was the wife and the sister of Jupiter. Because of her husband's endless infidelity, Juno is also known for her capacity for vengeance and jealousy towards his lovers, but she remained extremely loyal to her husband and their marriage endured.

Vesta

Keywords & associated symbols: Independence, virgins, self-sufficiency. The hearth, the fireplace, fire, home, cooking, focus.

Vesta is the goddess of the hearth and home. Though she had many suitors, she chose to remain single. She devoted her life to work and service, attending the eternal flame. This was not a sacrifice on her part. Remaining single and childless was her choice and allowed Vesta a certain amount of personal freedom. She is associated with a sister figure and with a maiden aunt, or with any woman who chooses independence, work and service. Known as Hestia in the Greek tradition, her name means 'hearth' and 'focus'.

Pallas Athena

Keywords/associated symbols: Daughter, wisdom, owls, the arts, war, the city of Athens.

Another 'virgin' goddess, Athena was born from the head of Zeus. She is the archetypal favourite daughter. Her Roman counterpart was Minerva. She is the goddess of wisdom, courage, inspiration, civilisation, law and justice, warfare, mathematics, strength, strategy, arts and crafts. She is typically portrayed as an armoured warrior with a serious and intelligent demeanour.

Jupiter

Keywords & associated symbols: Expansion, growth, growing up. Opportunities, aspirations, good luck, good fortune, risk-taking. Anything large. Philosophy, the law, religion. Extroversion, enthusiasm, generosity. The church, higher education, adventure, travel. Exploring, optimism, confidence.

When dysfunctional: Hubris, superiority complex, over-confidence, recklessness. Indulgence, a sense of entitlement, narcissism.

Metal: Tin

Ruling planet of Sagittarius and Pisces

Solar Orbit: 12 years

Synodic Period: 399 days

The Symbolism of Jupiter

Far larger than any other planet in our solar system, Jupiter represents expansion and growth and therefore symbolises anything big. Jupiter exudes confidence and is willing to take risks. Prone to excess, Jupiter can sometimes get out of hand. Not known for moderation, everything Jupiter does, he does on a grand scale. As the chief sky god, Jupiter/Zeus can be overblown and given to hubris. The typical Jupiter type is carefree and has more than their fair share of good luck.

Daredevils, risk-takers, preachers, evangelists and entertainers of all kinds are some of the characters aroused by Jupiter's boundless enthusiasm. Extroverts one and all, the typical Jupiter personality is the life of the party. They often live life in the fast lane, just like Jupiter, which has the fastest rotation speed of any planet. A full day on Jupiter is just 10 hours long. Jupiter is the ruling planet of Sagittarius and the traditional ruler of Pisces. Both signs can be prone to excess, but it's not just these signs that can evoke the energy of Jupiter. Anyone who embodies the Jupiter archetype can embellish stories, exaggerate and stretch the truth. They don't like to be restricted and will often flee the scene when confronted or challenged.

The Jupiter Cycle

The Jupiter year is about 12 Earth years long. It is at this age we start high school and our world expands. Adolescence and puberty start around this age and our social circle grows exponentially. Opportunities, learning and knowledge dramatically increase, and we begin to explore the wider world. There is a vast treasure of undiscovered information and territory out there and Jupiter urges us to experience it all.

Every 12 years, Jupiter will come back to its birth position. These Jupiter returns bring us opportunities for personal growth and further exploration. It's not just about exploring the world out there. Jupiter is also interested in the meaning of life and spiritual matters. Travel is said to broaden the mind, but Jupiter also fosters a sense of purpose. Journeys and pilgrimages offer both opportunities for personal development and spiritual growth. Spiritual retreats often appeal to Jupiter types, who are keen to expand their mind and knowledge.

Growth and expansion are the chief domains of Jupiter, who abhors restrictions of any kind. Jupiter grabs hold of every available opportunity. In all he undertakes, he's confident and enthusiastic.

Jupiter in Storytelling

In Stanley Kubrick's *2001: A Space Odyssey*, the spacecraft *Discovery One* is on a mission to investigate Jupiter. The 1968 science fiction epic was co-written by Arthur C. Clarke. Known for its ambiguous and symbolic narrative, the movie explores both the inner and outer reaches of space, inviting us to contemplate themes such as human evolution and the search for meaning.

In the 1988 movie *Big*, starring Tom Hanks in one of his first roles, 12-year-old Josh Baskin is trying to impress a girl at the local amusement park. He's told that he is too short to go on a carnival ride. Feeling rejected, Josh inserts a coin into a fortune-telling machine and makes a wish to be big. The machine dispenses a card saying, 'Your wish is granted'. The next morning, Josh has grown into an adult, but he is still a child at heart. He lands a job in developing and marketing toys. He meets a woman and begins to develop a steady relationship. At first Josh enjoys being 'big' but he misses his family and longs to return to his youth. Eventually Josh finds the fortune-telling machine again and is transformed back into a 12-year-old.

Who knows why the screenwriters chose the age of 12 for their main character, but it's perfect. It's the exact length of time it takes for the biggest planet to orbit the Sun.[2]

Saturn

Keywords & associated symbols: Limitations, restrictions, structure. Ambition, authority figures, the material world. Self-discipline, responsibility. Old age, time, antiques, boundaries, fear. The knees, bones and teeth. Governments, bureaucracy, conservatives, any chronic condition.

When dysfunctional: Fear, worry, depression. Clashes with those in authority, lack of discipline. Avoidance of responsibility, or taking on too much responsibility. Pessimistic, overly serious, strict, gloomy.

Metal: Lead

Ruling planet of Capricorn and Aquarius

Solar Orbit: 29 years

Synodic Period: 378 days

The Symbolism of Saturn

Saturn has a heavy feel to it. Its associated metal is lead. In life, we are often obliged to take on responsibilities and sometimes they can become burdensome. We must deal with schedules and manage time in an orderly way. These are the chores Saturn assigns to us. Government rules and regulations, and people in positions of authority whose job it is to administer them, evoke the Saturn archetype.

The mythic Saturn (Greek Cronus) was the lord of time. He was a Titan, from the old hierarchy of gods who ruled before the Olympian gods came to power. Saturn was a stern parental figure who swallowed his children so they would not usurp his power and overthrow him. His wife Ops/Rhea managed to save one child, Jupiter/Zeus. Eventually, Saturn had to step aside for his son Jupiter, who became the chief god. Yet Saturn wields formidable influence, imposing arduous tasks and hurdles.

For a very long time, the planet Saturn was the most distant known planet in the solar system and its traditional interpretation still holds true. Its vast ring system also speaks to the theme of boundaries and limitations.

Saturn rules Capricorn and it's also the traditional ruling planet of Aquarius. The Sun is moving through Capricorn and Aquarius at the coldest time of the year in the northern hemisphere, which is a clear reference to the coldness of Saturn, psychologically speaking, as well as the planet's remote distance from the Sun.

The Saturn Cycle

If you watch the nightly news, you will often hear reports of events concerning people aged 29. It happens so frequently, it's almost a daily event. These stories often feature individuals who have had brushes with the law, or been arrested. With an orbital cycle of 29 years, Saturn will lay down the law as it returns to its natal position when we reach this age, especially if we have been behaving irresponsibly.

At the age of 58 and at 87, Saturn will once again come back to its birth position, but it is the first Saturn return at 29, which typically resonates most profoundly. The Jupiter cycle is 12 years long and we've had two Jupiter returns before Saturn comes back. Jupiter can be like a young juvenile offender who has no understanding of responsibility and no self-discipline. But when Saturn comes along, we are taught a valuable lesson. Boundaries, rules, structures and systems are important. We need to come to terms with these aspects of life if we want to achieve anything worthwhile and lasting. There are no shortcuts. We must pay our dues. The age of 29 is when we often make key life decisions and commitments such as getting married, starting a family, establishing our own business, or making a big career move.

Every seven years or so we all undergo a Saturn square. You've probably heard of the seven-year cycle or the seven-year itch. This corresponds with Saturn squaring (and opposing) its birth position. These intervals mark significant rites of passage. At the age of seven, we become more self-aware, learning more about the rules and systems of society and what is expected of us. At 14, Saturn opposes its birth position for the first time and we encounter peer-group pressure. Puberty arrives and we try to fit into a social group and establish relationships. The age of 21 is a very important time when we venture out into the world on our own.[3] Throughout life, every seven years, we encounter the challenges of Saturn. Saturn helps us to become mature adults. Accepting our responsibilities and being self-disciplined are essential if we want to set and reach our goals.

Saturn in Storytelling

Countless stories explore Saturn's themes and symbolism. Charles Dickens' *Great Expectations* (1861) follows the life of Pip, an orphan who grows to maturity. Ambitious to climb out of his humble beginnings, Pip aspires to a higher social standing. The story explores themes of social class, austerity, gratitude and the journey we take from youth to maturity. Social injustice, hardship and adversity feature in John Steinbeck's *The Grapes of Wrath* (1939). In the 2008 film *The Curious Case of Benjamin Button*, we see the story of a man who ages backward through time. He begins life looking old and gradually becomes younger. Saturn's symbolism of time and aging is central to the narrative. In George Orwell's 1949 classic novel *1984*, Saturn's authority cannot be questioned. Every citizen must comply with the strict rules of the oppressive regime, which controls every aspect of life.

In the 1997 movie *The Ice Storm*, the weather is a metaphor for the coldness we see reflected in the characters' relationships. Set in 1973, at the time of the sexual revolution, there is a lot of sexual experimentation between the characters, but they are all rather disengaged from one another. There are no emotional connections between them. It takes the death of a child at the end of the movie to break the ice. In one way or another, all the characters in *The Ice Storm* are struggling with their own inner demons. They are stuck within the rules and structures of their traditional roles, but they are all in quiet rebellion, somehow trying to escape the reality of their mundane lives. After the 'key party' where the adults pair off for sex with different partners, Janey returns home alone. She curls up on her waterbed in a foetal position. While she sleeps, her son dies in the ice storm, electrocuted by fallen power lines. His body is discovered by her lover/neighbour, played by Kevin Kline. At the end of the movie, all the characters express their grief and begin to warm to one another in their shared tragedy. But Janey is not with them. We are left wondering how the death of her son will affect her.

Director Ang Lee uses a range of other symbols in the movie, such as keys (Chiron) and doors. Doors are associated with the Roman god Janus, the two-faced god of entrances and exits, beginnings and endings. The month of January is named after Janus, which is the month when the Sun is moving through Capricorn, Saturn's sign. The screenplay by James Schamus was based on a novel by Rick Moody. It won Best Screenplay at the Cannes Film Festival.

Chiron

Keywords & associated symbols: Wounding and healing, teaching and wisdom. Mentors and mentoring. The hands and the thighs. Keys.

When dysfunctional: Isolation, depression, feeling sorry for oneself, self-harm, chronic health issues.

Solar Orbit: 50 years

Synodic period: 358 days

The Symbolism of Chiron

Many people don't know there is an object in our solar system named Chiron. It was discovered in 1977. Chiron might be a captured comet or a rogue asteroid. It takes about 50 years to orbit the Sun in a highly elliptical orbit.

In myth, Chiron was the immortal son of Cronus (Saturn) and a nymph called Philyra. Rhea, Cronus' wife, interrupted his tryst with Philyra so Cronus transformed himself into a horse to escape detection. As a result, Chiron was born a centaur, half human, half horse. Both his parents abandoned him.

Later, Heracles accidentally wounded Chiron, shooting him in the thigh with a poisoned arrow. Because Chiron was immortal, he could not die and so he suffered immense pain. In attempting to cure himself, he developed a vast range of healing skills and became known for his knowledge and wisdom. He taught the healing arts to many others.

Eventually, Chiron was set free from his torment by renouncing his immortality. The glyph for Chiron is a key. This relatively new glyph is a stylised depiction of OK for 'object Kowal', which was the provisional name for Chiron when discovered by Charles T Kowal in 1977. The symbol of a key is a good fit for Chiron. Chiron's highly elliptical crosses the orbits of Saturn and Uranus. It is a gateway or bridge to the outer solar system. Keys unlock valuable treasures that are secured behind closed doors. The key is also a symbol of authority, in particular spiritual authority and it represents imprisonment and freedom.

The Chiron Cycle

The Chiron return happens to everyone around the age of 50 or 51 and signifies a time when health issues can emerge. Women usually go through menopause at this age. As we arrive at this time of life, we often have to manage issues with elderly parents. We also become more aware of the ageing process and our own mortality. Nevertheless, by the time we reach 50, in keeping with the wise centaur, we have usually reached a level of wisdom, self-acceptance and maturity, which elicits deep-seated healing and provides a sense of freedom. Coming to terms with our wounds and the arc of our life journey is part of Chiron's story and ours.

Because Chiron has a highly elliptical orbit, its squares and oppositions don't happen at the same time of life for everyone. It's the same with our wounds. They can be random and they can be accidental. The Chiron return universally signifies the journey of maturity and self-acceptance. Some wounds, whether physical or psychological, can remain unhealed; but Chiron enables us to share our stories and connect with others and these connections foster healing.

Chiron in Storytelling

In the 1959 movie *The Nun's Story* starring Audrey Hepburn, there is a long scene at the end of the movie involving keys and doors. The movie was developed from a book by Kathryn C Hulme; the screenplay is by Robert Anderson and directed by Fred Zinnemann.

All through the story, Sister Luke struggles with obedience to the church rules (Saturn). After graduating with high marks in her study of tropical diseases (Chiron), she hopes to be sent to Africa, but she is sent to work in a psychiatric hospital. A violent patient tricks Sister Luke into opening her cell door in violation of the rules. Eventually, Sister Luke goes to Africa, but she is often late for prayers and would prefer to be ministering to her patients or teaching her students. The long hours and her spiritual struggles make her ill and she develops tuberculosis. While accompanying a sick patient to Belgium, World War II breaks out and she is compelled to stay in Europe. When her father is killed, she can no longer continue to obey the church and cannot forgive the German enemy. She decides to leave the church. In the last scene, as she gives back her keys, a door automatically opens to the outside world. She is free to leave the convent and continue her work as a healer, no longer restricted by the Saturnian rules and regulations of the church.

Chiron's symbols and keys also feature in the *Shawshank Redemption* (1994) adapted from a short story by Stephen King. Andy is wrongfully imprisoned for the murder of his wife and her lover. He is innocent and while in prison, he behaves like a free man. No matter what befalls him, he always retains his free spirit. Andy becomes a mentor and teacher (Chiron) to other prisoners. He uses time to his advantage. He writes letters to the authorities (Saturn) asking for money and books for his library project. In one scene, Andy locks himself in the warden's office, but in doing so, he is free to express himself. He plays music over the loudspeakers so the other prisoners in the compound can listen and experience healing. As punishment, he is locked in solitary confinement, but the memory of the music sustains him throughout this ordeal. He reckons it was worth defying the authorities. Meanwhile, with the help of time (Saturn), Andy tunnels his way to freedom.

Mentors often feature in stories. The wise woman, or wise man, offers advice and helps the main protagonist on their journey. These characters teach from experience and share the lessons they have learned from their own healing journey.

The wounded healer is also a theme commonly explored in medical dramas such as television series *House* and *The Good Doctor*.

Uranus

Keywords & associated symbols: Freedom, rebellion, the future, independence and technology. Human rights, the unexpected, originality, eccentricity. Sudden changes, humanities, inventors and inventiveness, genius. Bohemians, anything unconventional. Knowledge, electricity and electrical devices. Science, science fiction, new discoveries, robotics. Metaphysics, progress, creativity, artificial intelligence.

When dysfunctional: Stress and anxiety, inability to cope with change, fear of the future. Inflexibility, rebellion, chaos. Spasms and electrical faults, anxiety, disruption. Unsympathetic, aloof, dogmatic or obstinate thinking.

Metal: Uranium

Modern ruler of Aquarius

Solar Orbit: 84 years

Synodic period: 369 days

The Symbolism of Uranus

Discovered unexpectedly in 1781, around the time of the Industrial Revolution and the French and American Revolutions, Uranus symbolises sudden change, freedom, human rights, science, technology and the future. Uranus is the modern ruling planet of Aquarius, as they share an interest in these innovations. The discovery of Uranus was a complete surprise, which overturned the traditional model of the solar system. The planet's axis of rotation differs wildly from any other planet, so it's totally original. This most maverick planet symbolises these rebellious qualities. Uranus is the only planet named after a Greek god.

Uranus (to avoid the potential giggles, astrologers tend to pronounce it you-rah-ness) has had a lot of different names. At first it was called 'George' after King George III, who was the British monarch at the time of its discovery. Then it was called 'Herschel' after the astronomer William Herschel, who first identified Uranus in March 1781. Many astrologers liken Uranus' energy to the god Prometheus, who is credited with creating the human race from clay. Prometheus then stole fire from the gods and gave it to humanity. But at this late stage, another name change for the rebel planet is unlikely.

Sometimes Uranus is pre-emptive and can jump the gun. Uranus delivers electrifying insights, propelling us forward with exhilarating momentum. This can sometimes lead to chaos if we overthrow everything we have built and developed with the help of Saturn. Burning those bridges can backfire if we act too hastily. Finding a balance between Saturn's rules and discipline and the rebellion and creative freedom of Uranus is one of the major challenges in life.

The Uranus Cycle

Uranus has an 84-year orbit, which corresponds to the approximate length of a human life. This can be divided neatly into four important life segments. At age 21, everyone has their first Uranus square when we symbolically gain our freedom and independence and get 'the key to the door'. Although the exact age for leaving home and striking out on our own can vary, the Uranus square at the age of 21 symbolises this important step. At this time of life,

Saturn is squaring its birth position too, which makes this period additionally challenging.

Uranus will oppose its natal position when we are going through the midlife transition at the age of 42. It's one of life's major challenges to be true to ourselves and at the same time manage our day-to-day responsibilities and obligations. Often there is a lot of stress and tension around the Uranus opposition.

As the Greek philosopher Heraclitus once said, 'Change is the only constant in life.' Changing careers, or partners, or lifestyles, is not uncommon at midlife. Returning to study is another popular choice. But these are external reactions to an inner feeling of disquiet and rebellion. If the Saturn-like structures we have built for ourselves are too limiting, or too onerous, or we have been constantly doing what others want us to do and not expressing our true nature, then Uranus can suddenly enter the scene, helping to make space for our creativity and self-expression.

Over time, we come to understand more about ourselves and become more aligned with our true nature. As we grow, consciousness and self-awareness develop. The Uranus cycle underscores this process, triggering external events and personal insights, which awaken us to who we really are.

At 42, Saturn is also making a hard aspect to its birth position. Midlife is often experienced as a time of crisis and rebellion and can herald a complete change in direction. Changes can happen because of external circumstances, or if we are feeling stuck, or both. Whatever happens, the Uranus opposition urges us to make big changes so our life better reflects our true self. The person we have become at midlife is probably quite different from the person we were at the age of 21.

At the age of 63, around retirement age, we encounter our second Uranus square and once again we undergo major life changes and adjustments. At 84, Uranus returns to the same position it was at our birth and we can view the arc of our life's journey.

Uranus wakes us up and can deliver radical changes. In my experience, Uranus is not usually wildly disruptive unless we are in dire need of a major shake-up. When that happens, it's like receiving an electrical shock. We suddenly see things in a totally new light and wonder how on earth we didn't see it before! This is especially true at 42 years of age. As Douglas Adams famously wrote in *Hitchhiker's Guide to the Galaxy*, 42 is the Answer to the Ultimate Question of Life, the Universe and Everything.

Uranus in Storytelling

In Greek mythology, Uranus is the personification of the sky, the son and husband of Gaia (Earth) and the father of Cronus (Saturn). Uranus locked his children away inside Gaia, who suffered in pain until she persuaded her son Cronus to rebel. Cronus castrated his father with a sickle, tossing his genitals into the ocean.

While Uranus fathered Cronus (Saturn), his son also overthrew him. As far as the sky god Uranus is concerned, the sky is the limit. He is the original father of all creation, but this mythic tale reminds us that the Earth and Saturn can curtail our freedom and creativity.

Many astrologers have likened Uranus to Prometheus, one of the ancient and powerful Titans who existed before the Olympian gods. In Olympus, Zeus/Jupiter, was the king of the gods and he withheld the knowledge of fire from humans. Fire was considered a divine power and Zeus feared that allowing humans to possess fire would empower them to challenge his authority. In an act of defiance, Prometheus stole fire and gave it to humanity, thus giving them the means to advance by providing them with warmth and light.

Zeus was furious at Prometheus for disobeying him. He punished Prometheus by binding him to a rock where each day, an eagle would come and eat his liver, which would then regenerate overnight. Prometheus endured this punishment for a long time until the hero Heracles (Hercules) eventually freed him.

Revered as symbols of human creativity and ingenuity, the quest for knowledge and the price one might pay for defying authority, both Uranus and Prometheus have inspired countless literary works. Mary Shelley's *Frankenstein* (1818) and HG Wells' *The Time Machine* (1895) explore how unchecked scientific advances can create a monster. The movie *Prometheus* is a 2012 science fiction film directed by Ridley Scott. Set in the late 21st century, it follows a team of scientists who embark on a journey to a distant planet in search of answers about the origins of humanity.

Neptune

Keywords & associated symbols: The collective unconscious, spiritual beliefs, the desire for meaning and belonging. Dreams, imagination, hallucinations, mysticism, spiritualism, psychics. Alcohol, drugs, anaesthetic, dementia. Magic, mystery, hypnosis, transcendence, self-sacrifice, idealism. Photography, music, film, illusion. Oil, gas, the weather, the ocean, seahorses.

When dysfunctional: Playing the victim, avoiding reality, mental illness. Disillusionment, depression, deception, drug and alcohol abuse. Delusions, conspiracy theories, scams, blind worship, cults.

Metal: Neptunium

Modern ruler of Pisces

Solar Orbit: 165 years

Synodic period: 367 days

The Symbolism of Neptune

Lord of the oceans and seas, Neptune is a mysterious figure, unfathomable and sometimes downright strange. Planet Neptune is a distinct blue colour, again suggesting the ocean's depths. Since its discovery, Neptune has become the modern ruler of Pisces. This is due to the obvious symbolic connection between the sign of the fishes and Neptune's governance of the ocean and other waters. Both Pisces and Neptune have an otherworldly feel to them. They also share an interest in spiritual matters, dream states and imagination, which is why modern astrologers were quick to recognise this link.

Dreams and other messages from the unconscious allow us to glimpse the magic and mystery of Neptune's realm and find inspiration. But Neptune is elusive. It's virtually impossible to capture its essence. Sometimes we can transcend the fuzzy space between consciousness and the unconscious, where magic happens, but we can never control it. Likewise, the ocean depths hold many mysteries we might never discover or comprehend. The ocean is as powerful as it is deep and mysterious.

The mythic Neptune/Poseidon has rulership over earthquakes and the weather. He would use his trident to generate storms and shake the Earth, so tsunamis and other natural disasters are part of his arsenal. He is associated with all sea creatures, especially dolphins and has a strong connection with horses. Neptune sometimes transformed himself into a horse and would ride a horse-drawn chariot across the sea. But these were not your average horses, they were fish tailed horses, known as hippocampi. Neptune's smallest known moon, discovered in 2013, is named Hippocamp.

This is the etymological origin of the word hippopotamus, or river horse. Hippocamp is also the Greek source for the part of the brain called the hippocampus. Interestingly, in dementia, this is one of the first parts of the brain to be affected, causing short-term memory loss and disorientation. Neptune symbolises these confusing and debilitating symptoms too.

Galileo spotted Neptune through his telescope in 1612, but in keeping with its elusive nature, he mistook it for a fixed star. Neptune was stationary at the time, which explains why Galileo recorded his observation as a star. Another 234 years elapsed before Neptune was discovered in 1846. Its discovery brought into consciousness a wave of interest in activities symbolic of Neptune, including hypnosis, spiritualism and impressionism, to name a few. If you are writing historical novels set in this era, these are just some of the Neptunian themes can include in your narrative.

The Neptune Cycle

Just like the mythic Neptune, the weather on Neptune is intense. It's incredibly windy and generates formidable storms. Wind speeds of over 2,000 kilometres per hour have been recorded. It takes 165 Earth years for Neptune to orbit the Sun just once. If you divide this into four parts, you will notice Neptune squares its birth position at the age of 41–2. At the same time, Uranus opposes its birth position and Saturn is also in hard aspect to itself. Is it any wonder we call this time of life the midlife crisis? While Uranus is busy shaking us awake, making us feel restless and urging us to change tack, Neptune is having almost the exact opposite effect, making us question everything and filling us with doubt and lethargy. Meanwhile, Saturn is piling on more and more responsibilities. At midlife, Neptune infiltrates our consciousness and we can feel disillusioned, unmotivated and depressed. We might be keen to make a change at this time of life, but what exactly do we want to do? Where are we going? What is life all about? What is my purpose? Why am I here? Neptune asks us so many questions, it can be difficult to find the answers, especially when we feel like we are engulfed in a heavy fog.

Neptune in Storytelling

There is a shapeshifting quality to Neptune. Shapeshifters are another key archetype often encountered in stories. As a writer, if you want to create a mysterious atmosphere, consider the symbols and themes linked to Neptune. Any story where water or the ocean plays a key role in your story will evoke the mysterious energy of Neptune.

Sometimes we should just let Neptune flow through us. Immersing our souls in nature, music and art are positive ways to work with Neptune and receive much-needed inspiration. Dreams, meditation and psychic impressions can guide us. Imagination inspires and informs the writing process.

Neptune offers incredible scope for writers to free themselves from the rules and confines of material reality and construct entire new worlds. In the 2010 movie, *Inception,* director Christopher Nolan uses elements of Neptune's symbolism to create a mind-bending story where characters enter and manipulate dreams. The film explores the boundaries between reality and dreams, illusion and truth and the power of the subconscious mind. The 2006 film *Pan's Labyrinth* explores a journey into a fantasy world to escape the harsh realities of life. In the 2001 cult classic, *Donnie Darko,* Donnie experiences strange visions and encounters a mysterious figure who guides him through a series of surreal events. The film explores themes of time travel, alternate realities and mental illness.

The fantasy genre is especially Neptunian. Whether set in the past, the future, or the present, fantasy is where we escape reality. Lewis Carroll's classic tale *Alice's Adventures in Wonderland* (1865) features dreamlike and illusionary elements that challenge Alice's notion of reality. In *The Little Mermaid* (1837) by Hans Christian Andersen, the mermaid longs to become human to be with the prince she loves. Neptune, as the ruler of the seas, holds power over her destiny and the story explores themes of sacrifice, love and the complexities of human desires. From classic movies like *Excalibur* (1981) and *Clash of the Titans* (1981), to JK Rowling's *Harry Potter* series, or the *Lord of the Rings* trilogy, in fantasy, there is always magic.

Pluto

Keywords & associated symbols: The underworld. Primal instincts. Power, transformation, survival. Death and rebirth, destruction and regeneration. Caves, secrets, hidden realm, darkness. Mines and miners. Atomic power. Fate, karma, obsessions. Wealth, plutocracies, spies.

When dysfunctional: Blaming others for our fate or actions. Allowing others to control us. Controlling behaviour, hoarding. Deep-seated fear, fear of death. Power struggles, paranoia, violence, greed, looting. Inability to let go, manipulation, emotional blackmail, sexual abuse, murder.

Metal: Plutonium

Modern ruler of Scorpio

Solar Orbit: 248 years

Synodic period: 366 days

The Symbolism of Pluto

Pluto was discovered in 1930, just as the world descended into the dark abyss of the Great Depression. Not long afterwards, fascism emerged, which led to the horror of World War II. Known as Hades in the Greek tradition, Pluto is the lord of the underworld. Pluto is an agent of transformation, death and rebirth and symbolises powerful forces beyond our control.

Pluto is the modern ruler of Scorpio and they share some common symbolism. In the northern hemisphere, the Sun is moving through Scorpio in autumn/fall when death and decay take place and hibernation commences. Nature is in retreat at this time of year and life moves underground. In the southern hemisphere, this is the time of year we experience the full flowering and rebirth of spring. This seasonal cycle reminds us that there is life after death.

Whenever we see Pluto prominent in a birth chart, you can be sure that the individual will be interested in exploring the unknown. Psychology, forensic medicine, detective work and even astrology itself are just some of the subjects where Pluto's passion for mystery and research can be applied.

The Pluto Cycle

Pluto's orbit is 248 Earth years long and because it has an elliptical orbit, it's not a simple matter to work out when the Pluto square and opposition will happen. While half a Pluto cycle is 124 years long, those who are in their 80s are experiencing their Pluto opposition about now. Some people will experience their Pluto square in their 30s, others in their 40s and others much later in life. This erratic pattern is consistent with the lack of control we have over matters of life and death. We all experience death at some point, including our own. What happens after death? The symbolism of Pluto speaks of rebirth and renewal. Science confirms that energy cannot be destroyed; it can only be transformed. Matter and energy are interconnected; in fact, science has shown us they are the same thing. Once the electrical energy in our hearts and brains is no longer present, where does it go? Does consciousness survive death? What is the soul? There are so many mysteries. Why does life exist at all? Pluto is interested in seeking answers to all these questions.

Pluto in Storytelling

In *The Divine Comedy* by Dante Alighieri, written in the 14th century, Pluto guards the entrance to the circle of avarice and greed. The journey begins with Dante, the narrator, lost in a dark forest of confusion and sin. Dante descends through nine circles of hell, then he enters purgatory where souls can atone for their sins. Here, sinners experience purification and redemption before they can ascend to paradise.

Transformation, death and rebirth are key components of Pluto's theme. Murder mysteries, underworld crime stories and a host of dark tales evoke the symbolism of Pluto.

In the insect world, a caterpillar transforms itself into a moth, or a butterfly. This theme is explored in the classic 1991 movie *Silence of the Lambs,* adapted from the 1988 novel by Thomas Harris. After being rejected for sex reassignment surgery, the serial killer Jame Gumb (also known as Buffalo Bill) is trying to transform himself into a woman by killing his victims and making a suit from their skin. He keeps moths at his house. A death's-head moth chrysalis is discovered in one of his victims' throats. FBI Agent, Clarice Starling (Jodie Foster) is sent to interview serial killer Dr Hannibal Lecter (Anthony Hopkins) to gain information about Buffalo Bill. Clarissa enters into a quid pro quo arrangement with Lecter to get his cooperation. She reveals a traumatic childhood experience of running away upon hearing the spring lambs screaming as they were slaughtered. The title, *Silence of the Lambs,* evokes these graphic themes. In the end, Agent Starling kills Buffalo Bill, but Lecter escapes and the audience knows a new chapter of killing is about to start.

Many books and films explore Plutonic concepts. In the 1999 movie *The Sixth Sense,* directed by M. Night Shyamalan, a child psychologist (Bruce Willis) treats a young boy who claims to see and communicate with the dead. The film explores themes of death, the afterlife and the emotional journey of the characters as they confront dark secrets. The 1990 movie *Ghost* starring Patrick Swayze and Demi Moore also explores Plutonic themes including loss, grief and the afterlife. The film examines violence and greed and their karmic consequences.

The Signs – Styles, Settings, Themes and Genres

When describing a particular zodiac sign, astrologers might say something like, 'Leos are proud' or 'Scorpios are secretive.' But we are not just talking about people who are born with their Sun in that sign; we are talking about the archetype itself or people who exhibit that sign's characteristics. Zodiac signs can describe the style or approach of your characters. For example, if Mercury is in Taurus, your character's communication style is going to be slower and more deliberate than if it is in Gemini, where they will probably talk non-stop. If Mercury is in Scorpio, for example, they are likely to excel at research, enjoy solving mysteries and be good at keeping secrets. If Mercury is in Virgo, they will especially notice details. Each sign has a ruling planet; some have two and some signs share a ruling planet. Signs and their ruling planets have something in common. As you explore the signs, keep in mind that each sign has symbolic links to their ruling planet, or planets.

In astrology, the Ascendant, or rising sign, describes the first impression or obvious characteristics of an individual. Psychologically, this is known as the persona. It's the mask a person wears. When you are developing your characters, consider their rising sign. Their persona could be very different from their Sun sign. Where is their Moon? The sign position of the Moon describes emotions and feelings. In this way, you can create complex characters that keep your readers guessing about their real nature and motives.

You can also use the signs of the zodiac as settings in your story. For example, Taurus might symbolise a forest or nature reserve, Sagittarius might represent the wide expanses of the outback and

Pisces might be an underwater world, or a cruise ship. Scorpio might be a secret passageway or a cave, Capricorn might be a large corporation or government department and Libra might be a beauty salon. Let your mind and imagination explore the vast array of symbols within the signs and the planets and let them guide you on your writing journey.

Aries

Polarity: Yang

Quality: Cardinal

Element: Fire

Ruling Planet: Mars

Symbol: The Ram

Positive Traits: Independent, assertive, honest. Courageous, pioneering, enthusiastic.

Negative Traits: Impulsive, reckless, headstrong. Selfish, aggressive, insensitive.

The Symbolism of Aries

The first sign of the zodiac, Aries, thrives on a challenge. Aries is the most honest, courageous and forthright sign. Brave and heroic, the typical Aries loves competition and is impatient for success.

Aries is the first sign because the Sun enters Aries at the spring equinox (in the northern hemisphere) around 21 March each year. Spring is a time of renewal and fresh growth. This is when the Sun is crossing the equator, heading north and we have equal hours of daylight and darkness everywhere on Earth.[4]

The archetypal action hero is an Aries and Mars is the ruling planet of this dynamic sign. Adventure stories, heroic quests and epic battles set the scene for Aries conquests. Winning matters. Aries likes to be first and he expects to win. Aries types believe that action speaks louder than words. The mix of the cardinal modality with the fire element fuels passion and creativity. It bolsters physical energy and elevates motivation.

Aries is a pioneer and an entrepreneur. These people don't waste time and live life to the full. Natural leaders, Aries types forge ahead, no matter what obstacles they face.

There are many types of hero; some are unwilling heroes who are forced by fate to take up a quest and, in the process, find out they are stronger than they knew. Whatever the journey, Aries people rush into battle, no matter the obstacles they might face. Material rewards don't motivate Aries. The typical Aries just wants to win.

Aries heroes are always willing to fight for an important cause. But no matter how brave and strong, heroes sometimes face defeat. The typical Aries will brush off defeat and downplay the value of any assistance they might receive along the way. Although not necessarily guaranteed victory, competition makes them stronger and fosters independence, which is highly valued for those who are ruled by hot-blooded Mars.

The typical Aries often jumps to conclusions. Impulsive by nature, they often lack patience. Aries types can be insensitive, aggressive and pushy, but they're unlikely to be vindictive. Their honesty and generosity make up for occasional bouts of selfishness or carelessness. Being headstrong can lead Aries types to occasional outbursts of anger, but temper tantrums are usually short-lived.

Aries people make great salespeople. They excel at selling themselves and their ideas. Apart from self-employment and creative occupations, Aries people are often drawn to daring and adventurous work, such as the police force or the military, though they are not so good at taking orders from those in authority. Aries takes the initiative in all things and does everything wholeheartedly. They like to be in charge, but are also chivalrous and romantic at heart. In relationships, the typical Aries wears their heart on their sleeve. They're passionate, fearless and driven. They're on a perpetual crusade, always ready for the next adventure, whatever it might be.

Aries in Storytelling

We can see Aries themes in any story involving a hero or heroic quest. Many stories like this follow the map of the hero's journey, quite literally. It's a common feature seen in the plethora of superhero franchises. Some of these stories are virtually identical and their heroes seem like plastic action figures. It's vital that protagonists have an inner life.

If you are using the standard map of the hero's journey as a template for your story, it's a good idea to add layers of complexity. Explore the inner workings of your hero or heroine. Dive deeper into their psychology. They might have a specific goal or task to fulfil but what is their internal motivation? What is their back story? What flaws do they have? Are they learning from their experiences? Stories are not just about action, but they are also about self-reflection and personal development.

The epic story of Jason and the Argonauts and their search for the Golden Fleece is a heroic tale that Aries people often relate to. In order to claim his birthright as the true ruler of Iolcos, King Pelias sent Jason on a seemingly impossible quest to claim the Golden Fleece. Jason immediately sets about assembling a crew of heroes and built the largest ship ever constructed, the *Argo*.

On the voyage, Jason and his crew face numerous trials and the *Argo* has to pass through treacherous clashing rocks. When they arrive at their destination, Jason is set even more tasks before he can claim the Golden Fleece. He has to yoke a team of fire-breathing bulls and use them to plough a field to be sowed with dragon's teeth. He then has to defeat the warriors who sprout from these teeth-seeds. Jason performed all the challenges set for him, but the King still refused to hand over the fleece and guarantee Jason's birthright.

With the help of the sorceress Medea and the goddess Hera (Juno), Jason eventually got hold of the Golden Fleece. Even then, he had more trials to face because King Pelias had no intention of honouring his promise to give up his throne. Eventually, Jason lost the support of Hera and betrayed Medea, who sought her vengeance. Having been through so many tests and trials, at the last hurdle, Jason dies alone and unhappy when a timber from the *Argo* falls on him.

This epic tale tells us there are often more tests and challenges in the hero's journey than the hero assumes when he first sets sail. In our own heroic quests in life, sometimes we must accept help from others and even then, when victory is at hand, that isn't the end of the story. Many heroes are brave and strong, and some have superpowers, but the average person is not Superman or Wonder Woman. While Aries is an enthusiastic and confident self-starter, ultimately there is a long road ahead for all of us and we should be grateful for the assistance we receive on our journey.

Well-known Aries Writers

Well-known writers born with the Sun in Aries include Quentin Tarantino, Maya Angelou, Hans Christian Andersen, Tom Clancy and Tennessee Williams.

Taurus

Polarity: Yin

Quality: Fixed

Element: Earth

Ruling Planet: Venus

Symbol: The Bull

Positive Traits: Determined, practical, sensual. Constructive, patient, thorough, resilient.

Negative Traits: Stubborn, controlling, materialistic. Obstinate, dogmatic, slow.

The Symbolism of Taurus

Taurus is a marriage of the fixed quality and the earth element, creating a formidable blend of determination, passion and resilience.

What Aries lacks in patience, Taurus makes up for in spades. Sensual, practical and constructive, Taurus is a builder, an engineer who is methodical and hands-on. Taurus wants to build something enduring to ensure lasting material security. The typical Taurus excels at using tools and can repair whatever needs fixing. You can trust Taurus to do a thorough job.

As the first earth sign, Taurus identifies, evaluates and establishes reliable standards. These benchmarks will evolve in the next earth sign, Virgo, where they will be honed and perfected and in earthy Capricorn, where they will be broadened and serve as guiding principles for social behaviour – so Taurus knows the importance of having a firm foundation upon which to build.

Loyalty is important to Taurus. Steadfast, enduring and intense, Taurus stands their ground. Taurus can be as stubborn as their symbol, the bull. It's difficult for Taurus types to adapt to changing circumstances and sometimes they can be rather inflexible, even pig-headed. It can take Taurus a long time to digest new information and recognise its value. They need time to evaluate the merits of what they encounter. Although its symbol is a bull, Taurus is a yin or feminine sign, ruled by Venus, the goddess of love and beauty. This might seem like a contradiction, but the feminine energy of this sign provides Taurus with a smattering of nuance to help balance its otherwise heavy symbolism.

The Sun is in Taurus at the full flowering of spring in the northern hemisphere, hence its association with fertility and the beauty of the natural world. With Venus as its ruling planet and natural affinity with the golden mean, the typical Taurus is passionate about planet Earth and all its living creatures. Plants, biodiversity and beauty go hand-in-hand. Many Taureans are passionately engaged in environmental projects and know a lot about flora and fauna. The typical Taurus wants to create something not only solid and enduring but also beautiful and sustainable.

Personal preferences and standards are determined by a process of evaluation. Once Taurus has formed an opinion and made a commitment, they stay the course and always follow through. They never give up. If they take on a particular task, they always complete it. They are very thorough and get the job done. The combination of the fixed quality and the earth element makes Taurus dependable and reliable, but when taken too far, Taurus can become fixated, stubborn and pedantic.

Being ruled by Venus, the planet of love, makes this sign incredibly tactile. They love good food and wine and appreciate fine art. Many Taureans are gifted in arts and crafts. Taurus rules the throat and neck so a good number of people with planets in Taurus have distinct voices and many are gifted singers.

As persistent as they are practical, Taureans have a firm set of personal standards that underpin and determine their actions. Some Taurus types can be overly materialistic, but most are just cautious with money. Taureans prioritise financial security, so you can trust they will make wise investments and not fall for get-rich-quick schemes or scams.

The bull is a potent symbol of fertility and power. We can 'take the bull by the horns' or, if taken to extremes, behave like a 'bully' or create havoc like 'a bull in a china shop'. The term 'bull market' describes advancement, profit and material gain, which is a chief priority for Taurus.

Banker, real estate agent, accountant, fashion designer, chef, masseur, beauty therapist, farmer, property developer, builder or tradesperson are just some of the many occupations where Taurean talents can be employed. They are dedicated and loyal employees, but they expect to be well compensated for their efforts. Taureans know their true worth.

Taurus in Storytelling

One theme associated with Taurus is money. Some stories focus on people who started out with very little and went on to achieve great success and wealth. These tales often reveal the perseverance, hard work and determination which led to prosperity. Other stories examine how people have managed when they have faced hardship and financial setbacks, highlighting the Taurean qualities of resilience and resourcefulness required to overcome these challenges. Some are cautionary tales involving greed, fraud and embezzlement, which offer valuable life lessons. Other stories explore social issues between the haves and have nots. Countless movies explore these themes including, *Wall Street* (1987), *Slumdog Millionaire (*2008*)*, *Margin Call* (2011), *The Wolf of Wall Street* (2013), *Crazy Rich Asians* (2018) and *The Big Short* (2015).

One mythic tale tells how Minos asked the gods for a sign they favoured his claim to the kingdom of Crete. Poseidon (Neptune) sent him a white bull to show his support. The condition was that Minos should sacrifice the bull to honour Poseidon, but after he became king, Minos decided to keep the magnificent beast for himself and sacrificed another bull of inferior quality. In retaliation, Poseidon caused the king's wife to lust after the bull. She mated with it and bore a hideous creature called the Minotaur, which had a human body and the head of a bull. It was hidden away in a labyrinth, where it feasted on human flesh. There is an important lesson in this story: when greed takes over, it can unleash dark forces.

Well-known Taurus Writers
Famous writers born with the Sun in Taurus include William Shakespeare, Harper Lee, Charlotte Brontë, L. Frank Baum and JM Barrie.

Gemini

Polarity: Yang

Quality: Mutable

Element: Air

Ruling Planet: Mercury

Symbol: The Twins

Positive Traits: Inquisitive, logical, versatile. Adaptable, observant, quick-witted.

Negative Traits: Superficial, argumentative, inconsistent. Erratic, contradictory, restless.

The Symbolism of Gemini

Gemini is a fast-paced, sociable and outgoing sign. Geminis are curious to know all about you and everything you are doing. They want to acquire more information, more data and more gossip and they like to share it with others. They are friendly and like to discuss a wide range of diverse topics.

Gemini is the sign of the twins and it has two distinct personalities rolled into one. Just when you think you understand them, they change. The air element combined with the mutable quality creates a lot of movement. Sometimes Gemini is blowing hot, sometimes cold, sometimes a gentle breeze, at other times a howling gale. You never quite know what to expect. The typical Gemini keeps everyone guessing.

Because there's usually only a few minutes separating their time of birth, the horoscopes of twins are virtually identical. Since they usually have the same upbringing, parental influence and share many experiences, their personalities often develop in similar ways. Astrological twins, those who are born at the same time, but who are not biologically related, can also have a lot in common. Whether biological twins, or cosmic twins, each soul has its own free will. We are each unique.

Geminis can see things from two sides and can go back and forth between two ideas or opinions in a split second. Just like Mercury, its ruling planet, Gemini is a trickster.

This sign is adept at all forms of communication. Writing is a natural function of Mercury, so Gemini types are keen to share their ideas. They are often prolific writers, but to complete long projects, they might need to develop more patience. Advertising and short stories are a good option for the typical Gemini mindset. They excel at marketing and networking. Geminis easily adapt to change and are always seeking new ways to engage with people. They have a natural flair for sharing information and they love gadgets and computer technology. Gemini's ruling planet, Mercury, orbits the Sun at breakneck speed. Geminis are like that too.

The weather is variable when the Sun is moving through mutable air sign Gemini. These seasonal changes in May and June are very much in keeping with the adaptable qualities of Gemini. Coping with variety and multitasking are second nature to this most versatile sign. Being social creatures, Geminis can become bored, restless and even depressed when alone.

Geminis have a love for learning and travel. They enjoy exploring new ideas and places and process information swiftly. Curious about everything and anything, they enjoy puzzles and games.

Though highly intelligent and keen to learn, Geminis can be easily distracted. Gemini is the chatterbox of the zodiac, always on the lookout for new information and people to talk to. Clever and alert, Geminis' restlessness can make it difficult for them to commit to anything for long periods. Keeping busy is vital. Problem-solving is second nature, assuming the work is interesting. Many Geminis work in the media and many are found in IT and public relations. Geminis also make good salespeople, actors, advertising executives, teachers, copywriters, translators – indeed any field where there is variety and communication.

They are always willing to discuss views openly and listen to others. They can put themselves in another's shoes and offer helpful advice, but they often have trouble dealing with emotions. While they are adept at communicating on an intellectual level, they are not so good at talking about feelings. Emotions are not rational and anything Geminis can't explain with reason and logic can make them uncomfortable. This tendency, plus their natural restlessness and their constant search for new experiences, means they can struggle to maintain steady relationships.

Gemini in Storytelling

To the Greeks, the twins were the mortal Castor and immortal Polydeuces (more commonly called by his Roman name, Pollux), who were half-brothers. When Castor died, Pollux insisted on sharing half his immortality with his brother so they could stay together forever. This mythic tale highlights the close bond between twins, but having different fathers, it tells us that twins are not exactly identical.

Writers frequently use twins to examine themes of individuality and duality. There are many stories involving twins where one twin is good and the other is evil. One of the earliest movies about evil twins is the 1946 film *The Dark Mirror*, starring Olivia de Havilland. It's a psychological thriller and film noir classic. It tells the story of Terry and Ruth Collins, one of whom has committed murder. But who is guilty?

Another very disturbing film about evil twins is *Dead Ringers* (1988) starring Jeremy Irons. In this story about twin gynaecologists, the brothers descend into madness. It's a twisted and quite horrific film and not for the faint-hearted.

We see a scary image of twins in the classic horror film *The Shining* (1980), co-written and directed by Stanley Kubrick. Twin girls stand side-by-side ominously in the hallway and invite young Danny to come and play with them, forever and ever.

The German word 'doppelgänger' originally referred to an apparition, or a ghostly image that was a harbinger of bad luck. In more general use, doppelgänger just means someone who resembles another. There is often a psychic bond between twins, but there is no evidence that twins are inherently evil. Nevertheless, it's an archetypal theme with a long and gothic history.

Well-known Gemini Writers

Famous Gemini writers include Anne Frank, Salman Rushdie, Arthur Conan Doyle, Walt Whitman and Harriet Beecher Stowe.

Cancer

Polarity: Yin

Quality: Cardinal

Element: Water

Ruling Planet: The Moon

Symbol: The Crab

Positive Traits: Protective, tenacious, caring. Intuitive, imaginative, empathetic.

Negative Traits: Moody, defensive, clinging. Anxious, self-pitying, overly sensitive.

The Symbolism of Cancer

If you watch a crab walking on the beach, they appear to be moving sideways. They know where they are going, but it seems like they are going about it the wrong way. Crabs have enormous claws and a tough outer shell and they use both for defence. Once those claws grab hold of you, they will not let go easily. If you have ever eaten crab, you will know the meat inside is sweet and tender. To get to that sweet meat, you first must break through that hard shell. Your average Cancerian is much the same. They look much tougher than they are. They are sensitive creatures, inside at least. But take a closer look and you find they are quite formidable. Don't underestimate their tenacity. The typical Cancerian is quite robust, but they don't feel that way inside. Cancerians are highly creative and imaginative creatures. They're also incredibly resourceful. Being a cardinal sign gives them strength of character and leadership potential.

The mix of the cardinal quality and the water element is like a flowing river that carves its way through the landscape on its journey to the ocean. It meanders, twists and turns according to the surrounding environment. The terrain it encounters defines its shape. Like a river, Cancerians bond to their surroundings. Security, both emotional and material, is important for the typical Cancerian. It helps them to know where they are going and to carve out their niche. Those who have a strong Cancerian theme in their birth charts are often found working in caring professions such as nursing, social work or counselling. They are also drawn to express themselves in creative occupations and enjoy hobbies like photography and cooking.

Cancer is a yin sign ruled by the Moon. Being a water sign, feelings are the primary method by which Cancerians navigate their world. Like the phases of the Moon and the tides, Cancerians are always changing, but this is not like the mental agility of Gemini. It's more internal and subtle, driven by emotions rather than logic.

Cancerians feel most at home, at home. When in their natural habitat, they are commonly found in the kitchen. Cooking and eating are favourite Cancerian pastimes. They are often very caring and protective of the people they love and are quite intuitive about the needs of others. They are known for their loyalty and devotion to family and loved ones. On the negative side, Cancerians can be prone to moodiness and are quite sensitive and easily hurt. They can also be possessive and clingy in relationships and can resort to emotional blackmail and passive-aggressive behaviour. The sensitive nature of Cancerian individuals can make them prone to worry and anxiety. They imagine worst-case scenarios, becoming consumed by fear and stress. They can have a deep-seated fear of rejection and worry about being abandoned or excluded, leading them to seek constant reassurance and validation.

Decision-making is one area where this sign can have occasional problems. All cardinal signs are action-focused and want to move ahead at the first opportunity, but for the Cancerian about to step in a new direction, the mood and feel and general ambience must be just right. They need to feel secure. When this is lacking, Cancerians can become moody and emotional; at least, that's what it can seem like to the observer. Cancer is an introverted sign and therefore, the typical crab needs time and space to consider their next move. Once they know how they truly 'feel' about their situation and have used their capacity to visualise and imagine the desired outcome, they will act decisively.

The Sun moves into Cancer in June at the solstice when it reaches the Tropic of Cancer at the start of summer in the northern hemisphere. This is the start of winter south of the equator. The Cancer ingress of the Sun brings the longest daylight hours up north (and longest night hours down south) and heralds this seasonal change. From our perspective on Earth, the Sun reaches its most extreme declination where it pauses before it changes direction. The word 'solstice' means exactly that, the Sun standing still. Whether north or south of the equator, the June solstice is a turning point in our annual seasonal journey.

Cancer in Storytelling

Cancer is the sign most associated with home and family. These stories explore family dynamics, especially the relationship between parent and child. In her 1977 book *My Mother My Self*, Nancy Friday points out the deep-seated challenges between mothers and daughters, which are rooted in biology. When a woman gives birth to a baby of the same gender, the maternal bond is amplified. There is a powerful sense of identification between mothers and daughters, but in order to grow to maturity, it's necessary for daughters to separate from their mothers and establish their own identity.

Some of the issues within this primary bond are explored in the award-winning 1990 movie *Postcards from the Edge*, based on Carrie Fisher's semi-autobiographical novel of the same name about her relationship with her movie-star mother, Debbie Reynolds. Fisher also wrote the screenplay. The film portrays the power struggle between the two women and charts a period in time when Debbie's career is waning and Carrie is trying to step out of her mother's shadow. Carrie Fisher suffered from bipolar disorder and at one time she received electroconvulsive treatments. As depicted in the movie, she was also addicted to cocaine and prescription medications. She and her mother were estranged for many years, but they eventually reconciled. Towards the ends of their lives, Carrie helped care for her mother. Debbie Reynolds passed away one day after her daughter Carrie.

Well-known Cancerian Writers

Famous writers born with the Sun in Cancer include Ernest Hemingway, George Orwell, Franz Kafka, Marcel Proust and the incredible Helen Keller. Though Helen Keller was blind and deaf, she was a prolific writer and learned several languages. She wrote 14 books and hundreds of essays and speeches. Keller's autobiography, *The Story of My Life*, was published in 1903 when she was just 22. It detailed her early struggles and education by her teacher, Anne Sullivan. It was adapted as a play by William Gibson and as a film, *The Miracle Worker* (1962). In keeping with this intuitive water sign, the first word Helen spoke was 'water'.

Leo

Polarity: Yang

Quality: Fixed

Element: Fire

Ruling Planet: The Sun

Symbol: The Lion

Positive Traits: Loyal, confident, creative. Generous, passionate, strong.

Negative Traits: Vain, bossy, self-centred. Stubborn, domineering, controlling.

The Symbolism of Leo

Leo is a combination of the fire element and the fixed quality, and it's ruled by the Sun. It radiates power and strength and contains an abundance of creative energy. The typical Leo has real 'star quality'. Creativity lies at the heart of the fifth sign of the zodiac. Leos like to show off their many talents, be it on stage, or in the sporting arena, or whenever an opportunity presents itself. They like to have an audience. Creativity is not just about artistry or self-expression; it can also manifest as procreation and a desire for a large family. Lions live in groups called prides and Leos are indeed proud creatures. Outgoing and optimistic, Leos take pride in their appearance and in their achievements.

Generous and affectionate, Leos make a powerful impression wherever they go. They enjoy being in charge. Leo the lion is a regal sign. It's always been associated with royalty and leadership. From the earliest times, the lion has symbolised strength and power. All the planets revolve around Leo's ruling planet, the Sun. It's at the centre of our solar system, which suggests Leo's natural position is centre stage. Leo types are used to everyone paying homage to their superiority. Leos value loyalty and disloyalty is not tolerated.

While an underdeveloped Leo is full of bravado and can be self-centred and vain, within Leo are the seeds of genuine confidence and success. The Sun represents consciousness, but consciousness evolves as we grow and develop. Before that, overconfidence can lead us into difficulties. Challenges and tests help us mature. Pride may come before a fall, but the fall can teach us important life lessons. This is especially true for Leo.

The marriage of the fire element and the fixed modality is a passionate combination. This type of fire burns constantly and is hard to extinguish. Fixed fire is like an eternal flame burning steady and strong, with endless fuel, like the Sun itself. Leos radiate warmth, have a positive, sunny outlook with lots of energy in reserve. Loyalty, love, passion and romance are at the heart of Leo and the typical Leo will seek a lifelong relationship. Leos love the idea of a big lavish wedding. This is partly because they have an opportunity to be the centre of attention on the special day and also because they love a grand celebration. Just like their feline relatives, Leos like to bask in the Sun.

Like the lion's mane, many Leos have beautiful hair. It's often long and thick and usually well groomed. Leo types enjoy visiting the hairdresser frequently and are loyal to the salon that follows their specific requests. Heaven help the hairdresser who messes up their Leo client's hair! When Leo gives an instruction and is paying for services, they expect the best. After all, they are royalty.

Imbued with many talents, the typical Leo thrives on praise and encouragement, but every sign of the zodiac contains positive and negative qualities and Leo is no exception. One negative trait is the tendency to be overly self-absorbed. The Sun is so big and radiant and dazzling, sometimes it can be difficult for Leo to focus on details. They much prefer to be in charge and delegate the small stuff to others. We all make mistakes, but when Leos make an error, their pride can prevent them from admitting they are at fault. But they are human, like everyone else.

Leo in Storytelling

The 1994 animated feature *The Lion King* is one of the most successful and popular stories of recent times. It was remade in 2019 and became a highly successful stage production seen by millions. It tells the story of young Simba as he grows from a cub to maturity and eventually claims his position as king and leader of the pride. Critics have commented that the story was inspired by, or even appropriated from, much older stories, including the Japanese animation *Kimba the White Lion* and an earlier, original story from Mali in Africa.[5] Sundiata Keita is known as the Lion of Mali and founded the Malian Empire in the 1200s, the largest kingdom in West Africa.

Christopher Vogler, the author of *The Writer's Journey* (1992), was a consultant on the animated Disney version and saw that elements of the hero's journey were incorporated into the script. As Vogler explains, in the beginning, we encounter the ordinary world of Simba, then he is called to adventure when his father tells him he must grow up and act responsibly before he can become king. Simba refuses the call and runs off with his friend Nala to explore the elephant graveyard. They are chased by a pack of hyenas. Mufasa rescues his son and Nala. Then we meet the shadow figure of Scar, Simba's uncle, who is working behind the scenes to claim the kingship for himself and has enlisted the help of the hyenas to attack Simba.

Then comes Simba's first big test, the death of his father. When Scar kills Mufasa, Simba escapes and finds new friends and allies. With their help, he confronts his uncle. Along the way, Simba encounters a range of archetypal characters – mentors, shapeshifters, tricksters and villains. Eventually, Simba returns to claim his kingship. Through his ordeal, he is transformed into a mature lion and eventually becomes king. Like Simba, to claim a position of authority, we must learn to be responsible. We should listen to the advice of wise mentors who can guide us towards our destiny.

As we see in the biblical tale of Samson and Delilah, long hair is a symbol of strength. Samson, whose name means 'man of the Sun', was incredibly strong. Betrayed by Delilah, Samson lost his power when she arranged for a servant to cut his hair while he slept.

Leo themes of royalty and hair also feature in the movie *Elizabeth* (1998). At the end of the film, the Queen's ladies-in-waiting cut her hair, transforming her into 'the Virgin Queen'. While she is giving away her youthful energy, she is also gaining power. Significantly, Virgo follows Leo in the zodiac. Elizabeth I, who was indeed a Virgo, tells Lord Burghley, she is now married to England.

Well-known Leo Writers

Famous writers born with the Sun in Leo include George Bernard Shaw, Emily Brontë, Aldous Huxley, Alexandre Dumas and JK Rowling.

Virgo

Polarity: Yin

Quality: Mutable

Element: Earth

Ruling Planet: Mercury

Symbol: The Virgin

Positive Traits: Analytical, precise, organised. Efficient, logical, industrious.

Negative Traits: Overly critical, anxious, nitpicking. Pedantic, aloof, workaholic.

The Symbolism of Virgo

Virgo is the sign of the virgin, but don't take this symbolism too literally. Self-sufficiency is what Virgo is all about. There is a hermit quality to the sixth sign of the zodiac. Virgo wants everything to be the best it can be and that includes perfecting itself.

The earth element combines with the mutable quality to create a practical yet adaptable character. Virgos have brilliant powers of analysis. Thanks to Mercury's rulership, Virgos can spot mistakes with precision and they are keen to correct errors as soon as possible. Virgos don't like to waste anything, including time. No other sign is as efficient as Virgo. They are mentally quick too; their ruling planet, Mercury, sees to that. Because of their capacity to focus and their ability to classify things, many Virgos are good at trivia. They often have broad general knowledge, plus one or two specialty subjects.

Another characteristic associated with Virgo is neatness. Some Virgos are not neat at all, but they do like to be organised. They have a kind of internal filing cabinet inside their brains. Virgos like to analyse the current situation and work out the best possible way to arrange things, so they will be easy to find when needed in the future. Virgos enjoy putting things in order, but most Virgos have better things to do than to spend all their time cleaning. Still, they are rather particular and choosey about all kinds of details, including grammar, punctuation, spelling, money matters, hygiene, diet, litter, health, work and relationships. Virgos can become overly critical and picky. They like to write lists and plan ahead, and they can become annoyed and frustrated when things don't go according to plan.

Career options are many and varied. Virgos are seriously dedicated to their work and need the mental stimulation it provides. But unlike Geminis, who prefer working with others, Virgos are more suited to solo occupations. In keeping with their mutable nature, over the course of a lifetime, the typical Virgo is likely to develop a range of skills, but they often specialise in a niche area. They prefer to learn about a subject thoroughly, to avoid making mistakes. When confronted by a problem, Virgos try to fix it before asking for help.

Apart from Mercury, Virgo is associated with several key asteroids. It's appropriate for asteroids to be symbolically connected to Virgo. They are small worlds, in keeping with Virgo's interest in details. Vesta was the goddess of the hearth and keeper of the eternal flame. She was the first-born of Saturn and the last to be regurgitated by her tyrant father after he swallowed his children. Although she remained a virgin, Vesta had several suitors, including Neptune, but she never had any intention of marrying. Like Queen

Elizabeth I, many Virgos choose to remain single. The typical Virgo doesn't need a relationship to feel fulfilled. Work is their primary focus. They like to keep busy and be of service. Another asteroid linked to Virgo is Ceres, who was the goddess of grain and crops. She is often depicted holding a sheaf of wheat. The Sun is moving through Virgo in late August and September, at the end of summer in the northern hemisphere, which is traditionally the time of the harvest.

Virgo in Storytelling

Virgo is associated with self-sufficiency. One classic film examining this theme is *Cast Away* (2000) starring Tom Hanks. After surviving a plane crash, his character, Chuck Noland, lives in isolation on a deserted island. In order to survive, he learns a host of skills and becomes totally self-sufficient.

A classic Virgo caricature is Felix Unger from *The Odd Couple* (both the 1968 movie and the 70s TV series). Felix is a neurotic neat freak and hypochondriac, who becomes roommates with the easy-going and messy Oscar Madison. This is a great example of the use of polarity in storytelling. When opposites attract or are thrown together by circumstances, stories can be filled with drama or with comedy.

Sir Arthur Conan Doyle's classic character, Sherlock Holmes, is well known for his attention to detail and his powers of observation and analysis in solving complex cases. Another Virgo-like detective is seen in the TV series *Monk* (2002–2009). Adrian Monk is a brilliant investigator with an exceptional eye for detail, but he also suffers from obsessive-compulsive disorder (OCD), which both helps and hinders his ability to solve crime.

Melvin Udall, in the 1997 film *As Good as It Gets,* also portrays notable Virgo traits. Jack Nicholson plays this socially inept novelist. His life takes a turn when he forms unlikely friendships with his neighbour and with a waitress.

One of my all-time favourite television characters is Victor Meldrew from the 90s British comedy, *One Foot in the Grave.* Victor Meldrew is a Virgo, always complaining about something. We know Victor is a Virgo because in one episode, he reads his horoscope in the newspaper. Annoyed by the endless trail of imperfections he encounters everywhere he goes, it seems like the world is against him. But Victor can't help himself. He tinkers and tweaks and often ends up creating more chaos with his fiddling. Along the way, he annoys the hell out of everyone, especially his wife and his long-suffering neighbours. Victor Meldrew is a great example of how you can exaggerate astrological traits to create a caricature.

Victor's creator, writer David Renwick, was also born under this meticulous sign. David knows what it's like to be a Virgo. It seems he drew on his personal experience to create a range of hilarious situations designed specifically to annoy his main character.

Well-known Virgo Writers

There is no shortage of successful Virgo writers. They include Agatha Christie, Roald Dahl, HG Wells, Mary Shelley, Stephen King, Leo Tolstoy and the creator of *Game of Thrones,* George RR Martin.

Libra

Polarity: Yang

Quality: Cardinal

Element: Air

Ruling Planet: Venus

Symbol: The Scales

Positive Traits: Diplomatic, fair, sociable. Stylish, charming, idealistic.

Negative Traits: Indecisive, superficial, submissive. Inconsistent, fickle, vain.

The Symbolism of Libra

When the Sun enters Libra at the second equinox of the year in September, it marks the start of autumn/fall in the northern hemisphere and the start of spring below the equator. Daylight and darkness are again equal. Libra is the sign of the balance, or scales. It's the only inanimate symbol in the zodiac and it symbolises equality, fairness and justice.

As the seventh sign, 180 degrees away from independent Aries, Libra is the primary sign of relationship. Those with a strong Libran theme are keen to consider other people's values. Personal relationships are the first step towards engaging with the wider community and Libra is keen to connect with people from all walks of life. Whenever a discussion seems to be too one-sided, Librans will always listen to others' opinions. They can see all sides of a problem, are adept at networking and they make excellent diplomats and mediators.

Venus is Libra's ruling planet, so harmony and beauty are just as important as relationships. Having a set of principles and standards is a key attribute for the typical Libran. Unlike fixed Taurus, where values tend to be set in stone, cardinal Libra is constantly evaluating and assessing and looking for consensus.

It's impossible to please everyone, but this life lesson can be a long time coming for some Libran natives. If unable to make up their mind, they can end up on a constant mental see-saw. Other people can find this Libran tendency frustrating because it is often difficult to know where they really stand.

Because relationships, equality and fairness are high on the Libran agenda, decision-making can be tricky. As a cardinal sign, commitments and taking action are important, but Librans can be torn between options, constantly weighing up the merits of various scenarios and their potential outcomes.

All air signs are extroverted (yang), so communication and social engagement are vital to Libran wellbeing. Although Libra is a yang or masculine sign, it's governed by a feminine planet. Venus seeks harmony in relationships, but as a cardinal air sign, Libra is also driven to achieve. This can create an inner dilemma, for how does one cater to everyone and at the same time fulfil one's own ambitions?

Apart from Venus, Themis is another goddess associated with Libra. She was the goddess of divine law and order. Themis is often depicted wearing a blindfold, holding the scales of justice and a sword. She governs the laws of civilised society and instructs humanity in matters of justice, morality, etiquette, hospitality and social conduct. Libra values all these qualities.

Juno is another goddess linked to this sign. Juno was the wife of Jupiter and was always loyal to her husband, despite his constant infidelities. Minerva/Athena, the beloved daughter of Jupiter/Zeus, is also associated with Libra. Clever and impartial and the goddess of wisdom and the arts, her symbol is the wise owl. She was a cultured goddess, an intellectual who was in every respect the equal of men. She involved herself in politics and in war.

Librans enjoy spending time and money on their appearance. They are keen to make a good impression, are usually impeccably groomed and have good manners. Impressions count. They are popular, charming and gracious. Librans want to bring people together and the way to do this is to create an atmosphere that attracts support for whatever cause or injustice they are working to resolve. Whether taking on the job of union delegate to ensure their colleagues are treated fairly, raising funds for a peace mission, or campaigning for animal rights, fair play and justice are most important. Whatever the problem, Librans know that equality and justice can be restored if only people would make the effort. Librans are suited to careers in politics, law, social services or law enforcement. They are also found in the beauty industry, artistic fields, interior or graphic design, customer service and public relations.

Libra in Storytelling

Romance and romantic comedy are genres we can associate with this sign. There are countless romantic tales; some are light-hearted comedies and some are tragedies. They illustrate the many twists and turns we take on our journey to find love. From classics like Shakespeare's *Romeo and Juliet* (1597) and Charlotte Brontë's *Jane Eyre* (1847) to films like *When Harry Met Sally…* (1989), *Love*

Actually (2003), or *The Holiday* (2006), there are endless variations on this theme. They speak to the complexity of personal relationships.

Legal dramas are another Libran theme. A host of television programs and movies explore this material. Long-running shows like *Law & Order*, *The Good Wife* and *Suits* speak to the popularity of this genre and our collective desire for justice.

The bestselling novelist John Grisham was a lawyer and politician before he became a writer. Many of his books have been turned into highly acclaimed movies including, *The Firm* (1993), *The Client* (1994), *The Pelican Brief* (1993), *The Rainmaker* (1997) and *A Time to Kill* (1996). They have become classics. Grisham is incredibly prolific. Apparently, every year on New Year's Day, he starts writing a new book. He writes every morning until lunchtime and completes each new book by July.[6]

Don't be discouraged if you are feeling intimidated by his success. 28 publishers rejected his first book, *A Time to Kill*, before it was published in 1988. Not one to give up (his Sun and Mercury are in fixed sign Aquarius), Grisham began writing his second book the day after completing his first.[7] His second book, *The Firm*, stayed on the *New York Times* Best Seller list for 47 weeks.

Well-known Libran Writers

Writers born with the Sun in Libra include Oscar Wilde, F Scott Fitzgerald, Arthur Miller, Truman Capote and TS Eliot.

Scorpio

Polarity: Yin

Quality: Fixed

Element: Water

Ruling Planets: Mars and Pluto

Symbol: The Scorpion

Positive Traits: Passionate, resilient, probing. Determined, resourceful, loyal.

Negative Traits: Controlling, jealous, suspicious. Distrustful, vengeful, manipulative.

The Symbolism of Scorpio

Scorpio is a combination of the fixed quality and the water element. Think ice. Large icebergs float with most of their mass under the surface, hidden from view. Danger lurks below. But that's only part of the Scorpio story. Although they like to keep a large part of themselves hidden, Scorpios are incredibly passionate and intense.

When Pluto was discovered in 1930, it was incorporated into the astrological pantheon and assigned co-rulership over Scorpio. Before that, Mars was the ruling planet of both Aries and Scorpio. These days, both planets are generally assigned to Scorpio, but even astrologers who prefer the traditional ruler Mars can't dismiss the symbolism shared by Pluto and Scorpio.

Mars and Pluto are both symbols of strength and power. Mars is the red planet, but the surface of Pluto has a distinctive dark-red hue as well. The inherent energy of Pluto is in keeping with a deep crimson colour. Pluto/Hades is the lord of the underworld, ruling over the souls of the dead. He has a magic helmet of invisibility. Just like Pluto, Scorpios like to be incognito.

Scorpio is a water sign and is therefore sensitive, emotional and imaginative. Despite its reputation for inflicting wounds, Scorpio usually only uses its immense power and emotional strength for defence.

Scorpions are arachnids. They have a sting in their tail and some of them can kill you. But most scorpion stings are not lethal, just very painful. Scorpions can survive in extreme environments like deserts and they can be frozen overnight and revived when thawed out the next day.[8] The oldest scorpion fossil discovered to date is around 420 million years old. They know how to survive. They can live without food or water for more than a year. Scorpio natives are survivors too. No matter what they endure, the typical Scorpio has the in-built capacity to emerge seemingly unscathed and they are more than capable of reinventing themselves. If necessary, Scorpios can push themselves to the edge of human endurance. They are masters of the art of both survival and transformation.

At the dark end of this intense zodiac sign, we see some of the grosser aspects of human behaviour, which normally stay hidden in the shadows. The unconscious contains not only the shadowy repressed elements of the psyche, but is overflowing with vast stores of beautiful treasures. Scorpios intrinsically understand the scope and depth of every archetypal theme and can freely access the wealth of material and untapped resources within.

Delving into mysteries and exploring the unconscious are natural pastimes for Scorpios. They have a real instinct for uncovering the truth. They're passionate about research and are often involved in forensic studies, counselling, healing, psychology, medicine or in occupations connected with death. For many Scorpios, themes of birth and death often go hand-in-hand.

The law of karma is something all Scorpios intrinsically understand. What goes around comes back around and for Scorpios, this often happens more immediately than with other signs.

Fated events are common among Scorpio natives, who often undergo a process of regeneration. Like a serpent shedding its skin, Scorpios often have to sacrifice something of themselves in order to grow. These experiences forge a rare depth of understanding and insight into people and life.

Scorpio in Storytelling

The shadow archetype is a powerful motif explored in the 1886 gothic novel *The Strange Case of Dr Jekyll and Mr Hyde* by Robert Louis Stevenson. The shadow is particularly associated with repressed aspects of the personality. This classic tale explores the struggle between good and evil.

Personally, I love a good murder mystery and the sheer number of books, films and TV programs created in this genre reflects their power to fascinate. Psychological thrillers and gothic horror tales are also associated with this sign. Scorpio writers and audiences enjoy plumbing the depths of the human psyche to explore what motives lie at the heart of these dark tales. Scorpios enjoy probing life's mysteries. Anything unknown is endlessly fascinating to Scorpio and the fixed nature of this sign keeps them passionately engaged. All Scorpios love research, which is a great asset for Scorpio writers.

Another aspect of Scorpio is the underworld themes we often see depicted on the screen, like organised crime. Countless films and TV shows have explored the dark underbelly of crime syndicates with their brutality and violence. With no regard for the law, they will do whatever it takes to make money, usually through shady means such as prostitution, gambling and drugs. Exploitation and blackmail are often employed to exert control.

Film noir is a favourite genre of mine. The style and themes of these classic movies from the 1940s and 1950s are haunting and magnetic. *Double Indemnity* (1944) starring Fred MacMurray and Barbara Stanwyck is a classic in the film noir style. The movie was co-written by Raymond Chandler and Billy Wilder and based on a novella by James M. Cain (1936). Cain also wrote *The Postman Always Rings Twice* (1934). Wilder directed *Double Indemnity*, which co-starred Edward G. Robinson as Neff's boss, an insurance investigator. The movie is full of great one-liners. The fabulous dialogue was mostly written by Chandler.

Tempted by the seductive perfume and alluring charm of femme fatale, Phyllis Dietrichson (Stanwyck) insurance sales agent Walter Neff (MacMurray) agrees to help her kill her husband for the insurance money. Eventually, the lovers have a falling out and Neff confesses to his crime. The film is told in flashback. In the first scene, Neff is seen bleeding from a gunshot wound and begins recording his confession on a dictaphone at his office.

Sex and sexuality are another subject connected to Scorpio. Manipulation and revenge are also part of the Scorpio arsenal. We see these themes explored in the 1988 movie *Dangerous Liaisons*. Christopher Hampton won an Academy Award for his screenplay. Glenn Close was nominated for Best Actress and the film was nominated for Best Picture. She also starred in the critically acclaimed 1987 movie *Fatal Attraction*, another classic scorpionic tale of passion and obsession.

Well-known Scorpio Writers

Well-known writers born with the Sun in Scorpio include Sylvia Plath, Fyodor Dostoevsky, Dylan Thomas, Bram Stoker and Margaret Atwood.

Sagittarius

Polarity: Yang

Quality: Mutable

Element: Fire

Ruling Planet: Jupiter

Symbol: The Archer

Positive Traits: Generous, enthusiastic, adventurous. Open-minded, optimistic, lucky.

Negative Traits: Careless, flighty, restless. Reckless, irresponsible, tactless.

The Symbolism of Sagittarius

There are several diverse concepts and themes connected to Sagittarius. As a centaur, with the upper body of a man and lower body of a horse, there are obvious links to Chiron, but Chiron was the only centaur who was wise. Sagittarius has a lot in common with the tribes of other mythic centaurs, who were the wild party animals of the Greco-Roman pantheon. This inherent duality presents us with two distinct types of Sagittarians: one is wild, the other is wise.

The myth of Chiron highlights the noble and selfless qualities associated with this sign, emphasising its potential as a compassionate healer and teacher. Chiron symbolises the pursuit of knowledge, the power of mentorship and the willingness to endure personal suffering for the greater good. Chiron's story serves as a reminder of the transformative and influential role mentors and teachers can play in shaping the lives of others. Teaching and higher education are themes associated with this ninth sign of the zodiac, along with religion and spirituality.

Jupiter rules Sagittarius, so there is a feeling of outward confidence and optimism intrinsic to this sign. There is a fun-loving, adventurous spirit within the typical Sagittarian. Jupiter is the largest planet in our solar system, so Sagittarians have an expansive view of the world, which accounts for the spiritual mindset and sometimes religious outlook.

Some Sagittarian types are overly extravagant, indulgent and reckless. When taken to extremes, the archer can be irresponsible, like a young adolescent who thinks they are bulletproof. We consistently find risk takers and daredevils within this archetypal group. Often high-spirited, Sagittarians act on impulse and take advantage of all opportunities. If no opportunity presents itself, they will go looking for one. Sagittarians can become easily bored. They like variety and are keen to explore. Exploring can mean travelling to far-off destinations, or inner musings to broaden the mind.

Sagittarius is a mix of the fire element and the mutable quality. It's outgoing, extroverted and adaptable. This type of fire can spread quickly and scorch the Earth, but any damage Sagittarius might cause is usually accidental. They are often outspoken and enjoy their independence. Like wild centaurs, they are keen to roam free and don't tolerate being hemmed in or restricted. Their adventurous spirit takes them wherever they choose to go.

Because of their optimism, they typically see only the best in others. They assume things will turn out for the best and they usually do. When difficulties arise, or when they are forced into a situation that boxes them in, they will often flee the scene and make a fresh start elsewhere. They're generous with their money and time and always willing to help others.

Sagittarians can be accident-prone. There are several reasons for this. Firstly, they have an adventurous nature; secondly, they tend to overestimate their ability to do things; and thirdly, they don't excel at managing the material world. Even when accidents happen, which can be fairly frequently, there often turns out to be a fringe benefit attached. At the very least, they will have an interesting story to tell.

The typical happy Sagittarian is the life of any party. But their natural exuberance, when combined with stimulants, can lead to excesses of all kinds. If something is good, then more of it must be better, right? Well, no, but moderation is not a word in the Sagittarian vocabulary.

On the negative side, Sagittarians can sometimes display a complete lack of tact. This is because of their straightforward approach to just about everything. They can be brutally honest and can unintentionally offend others with their frankness. Their love for freedom and adventure can make them so restless it can lead to difficulty in establishing long-term relationships.

Sagittarius in Storytelling

The figure of the centaur is half-horse and half-human. Some are wild creatures and some, like Chiron, are civilised and wise. Some horses are wild and some are tame. Stories involving horses often explore these differences – some examine cultural differences; others compare the exuberance of youth verses the wisdom of maturity; and some bear witness to the horrors of war versus the day-to-day activities of a peaceful life. Filmmaker Steven Spielberg is a Sagittarian. He's a director, writer and producer. Many of his films explore archetypal themes associated with this sign, such as *Close Encounters of the Third Kind* (1977), *Raiders of the Lost Ark* (1981), *E.T. the Extra-Terrestrial* (1982) *and Jurassic Park* (1993). While many of his movies are adventure stories, they also contain spiritual elements.

Spielberg directed the 2011 film *War Horse*. The movie is based on the 1982 novel of the same name by Michael Morpurgo, which was also adapted into a successful stage play. The film portrays the heart-wrenching journey of a horse named Joey during World War I.

Joey is raised by a teenage boy named Albert Narracott who develops a deep bond with Joey. But when World War I erupts, the family is forced to sell Joey to the British cavalry. Albert is heartbroken over losing his beloved horse. He joins the army, hoping to find Joey and bring him home. Joey experiences the horrors of war and serves on both sides of the conflict, ending up with the German army. Despite the challenges and dangers he faces, Joey remains resilient, displaying courage and determination to survive and return to his beloved Albert. The film highlights the enduring bond between humans and animals, amid the horror and devastation of war.

Other horse stories include *Black Beauty* by Anna Sewell. First published in 1877, the story examines kindness, cruelty and compassion. The 1998 film *The Horse Whisperer* also explores the powerful connection between horses and humans and the healing power of Chiron.

Well-known Sagittarian Writers

During his life, Sagittarian writer and humourist Mark Twain travelled widely. His enormous body of work includes a host of travel features. Many of his best-loved books are adventure stories, such as *The Adventures of Tom Sawyer* (1876) and *The Adventures of Huckleberry Finn* (1884). Other writers born with the Sun in Sagittarius include Jane Austen, Emily Dickinson, CS Lewis, Louisa May Alcott, George Eliot and the prolific screenwriter, Dalton Trumbo.

Capricorn

Polarity: Yin

Quality: Cardinal

Element: Earth

Ruling Planet: Saturn

Symbol: The Water-Goat

Positive Traits: Reliable, diligent, industrious. Patient, dependable, ethical.

Negative Traits: Pessimistic, anxious, negative. Austere, materialistic, authoritarian.

The Symbolism of Capricorn

The water-goat is a mysterious creature with the upper body of a goat and the lower part of a fish. This symbol connects Capricorn to the environment and reveals a softer side not immediately apparent. Goats climb mountains, but having a fish's tail suggests deeper and more mysterious traits hidden beneath the surface.

While Capricorns often possess an ambitious streak, sometimes leading to materialism, their conservative nature frequently manifests as a desire to conserve and preserve the environment. Many Capricorns have a deep respect for planet Earth and take their environmental responsibilities seriously. Many Capricorns are committed environmentalists.

The typical Capricorn honours past traditions and the lessons learned from history. With Saturn, the lord of time as their ruling planet, historical novels and biographies have special appeal. Capricorns respect their elders, but when others are not behaving ethically, Capricorns will set the record straight and stand up to those in positions of authority. At the very least, they set high standards, which can put others to shame.

The pairing of the cardinal quality with the earth element is a formidable combination. Practical yet driven, Capricorns want to achieve something useful and lasting. Like other earth signs, Capricorn is a yin sign, more introverted than extroverted; therefore, they attain success and achievement through methodical processes. They are patient and diligent.

Capricorns are self-motivated and cautious in their approach to life. Ruled by Saturn, they are willing to dedicate their energy and effort over a long period to attain the desired result. Their goals can be lofty. Capricorns like to be in charge and naturally aspire to positions of authority. Career-wise, they are often drawn to fields which offer stability, financial security and opportunities for advancement. They are likely to excel in business, finance, law, politics, engineering, or any occupation that requires a strong work ethic and a strategic mindset. While the trend these days is to change jobs and professions frequently, the typical Capricorn will continue to work diligently for years for the same organisation. Some Capricorns will establish their own businesses and those who do will work hard to make it a success. However, many Capricorns prefer the security of being part of a large organisation where they can rise through the ranks. Capricorn is the tenth sign of the zodiac, naturally positioned at the midheaven, which symbolises the pinnacle of human achievement. Capricorns aspire to positions of leadership. They always put duty before pleasure. To achieve success, they know one must be dedicated, thorough and most of all, disciplined.

Boundaries and complex systems are a natural fit for Capricorns. They respect old methods that have stood the test of time. To achieve results, they know it's vital to have a plan. Capricorn is the architect of the zodiac. One must lay a firm foundation and, importantly, get the right permits. There are rules one must follow. Capricorns never take shortcuts. The typical Capricorn is thorough and always behaves with integrity. They are dependable and skilled at managing and organising large-scale projects.

Sometimes austere and frugal, Capricorns avoid extravagance. They are conscientious and seek to minimise waste, excess and unnecessary consumption. They often adopt strict habits and routines, demonstrating a firm commitment to their goals or values. To reap, one must sow. It's normal for Capricorns to undertake tasks involving enormous effort because they understand the long-term payoff.

In relationships, the water-goat seeks security and stability too. They want a lifelong commitment. Sometimes they can seem aloof, but they are gentle-hearted and affectionate when you get to know them. Deep down, beneath the surface, there is that fishtail and a capricious, fun-loving side that likes to make a splash now and then.

Capricorn in Storytelling

Goats appear in a range of stories and myths. The term 'scapegoat' comes from an ancient ritual where a goat was chosen to carry the sins of the community. Goats were sacrificed or sent into the wilderness, thereby cleansing people of their wrongdoings. A range of stories explore this theme.

In *Animal Farm* (1945) by George Orwell, the cunning and power-hungry pig, Napoleon, blames Snowball for all the problems on the farm, making Snowball a scapegoat. In *The Scarlet Letter* (1850) by Nathaniel Hawthorne, Hester Prynne is publicly shamed and forced to wear a scarlet letter 'A' on her chest as a symbol of her adultery. She becomes a scapegoat for the judgement and hypocrisy of the puritanical society. *The Crucible* (1953) by Arthur Miller, set during the Salem witch trials of 1692, examines the allegations of a group of girls who accuse innocent people of witchcraft, leading to their convictions and executions. Those accused become scapegoats for the girls' lies and the community's fear. *The Grapes of Wrath* (1939) by John Steinbeck tells the story of Tom Joad, who becomes a scapegoat for a crime he didn't commit, highlighting the struggles of the poor and marginalised.

In Greek mythology, Pan is the god of shepherds and flocks. A satyr, Pan is often depicted with the legs, horns and beard of a goat. He represents the untamed and wild aspects of nature and also the capricious qualities hidden within Capricorn.

Other stories associated with Capricorn themes include *A Christmas Carol* by Charles Dickens. This classic tale, first published in 1843, follows the story of Ebenezer Scrooge, a miserly old man, who is visited by three ghosts on Christmas Eve. These visitations eventually transform Scrooge, healing his heart and softening his attitude towards others.

Well-known Capricorn Writers

Writers born with the Sun in Capricorn include JRR Tolkien, Edgar Allan Poe, JD Salinger, Susan Sontag and Simone de Beauvoir.

Aquarius

Polarity: Yang

Quality: Fixed

Element: Air

Ruling Planets: Saturn and Uranus

Symbol: The Water-Bearer

Positive Traits: Friendly, original, humanitarian. Scientific, progressive, idealistic.

Negative Traits: Intolerant, opinionated, cold. Stubborn, unsympathetic, detached.

The Symbolism of Aquarius

Aquarians can be difficult to categorise. There's really no such thing as a typical Aquarian. The electrical energy of Uranus animates some Aquarians to a high level of genius. They can be quite eccentric and can have a mad professor lurking within. Aquarians are among the most intelligent beings on the planet, but sometimes they are completely absent-minded. Other Aquarian types are far more saturnine. They are serious folk who are far more grounded and, like Capricorn, always follow the rules.

'Aqua' is Latin for water, which is why this sign is sometimes mistaken for a water sign. Aquarius is not a water sign; it's an air sign, but there is a lot of water within its symbolism. The sign of the water-bearer speaks to the process of purification. The symbol of a human figure pouring forth water from an urn suggests cleansing, or washing away impurities. February is the time of year when the Sun is in Aquarius. 'Februarius mensis' from the Latin means 'month of purification'.[9] The water-bearer also symbolises sharing knowledge, which is another key attribute of this sign.

All over the globe, there are prevailing winds. The wind is free to blow in a variety of ways, hot or cold, gentle breeze, or howling gale and like the wind, Aquarius likes to be free. Atmospheric currents drive our weather systems, but the weather is always changing, especially these days. It's likely many of the scientists working hard to generate solutions to climate change have Aquarian signatures in their charts. The combination of the air element with the fixed quality creates a bit of a contradiction, for air is never still. Even when the wind is not blowing, air is always in motion, circulating around us, but fixed energy is determined to stay put. It's steadfast and unwavering. This inherent contradiction can give rise to extremes. Aquarians are usually open-minded, but they can also be very dogged and unwilling to compromise. Air makes them excellent communicators, but their fixity can foster strong non-negotiable opinions.

Community engagement and teamwork appeal to Aquarians. They enjoy being part of a group and connecting with people who share a common objective. Even so, they are very independent and don't hesitate to forge ahead on their own. The duality often seen in this sign is also because it has two ruling planets, Saturn and Uranus, which are very different. Saturn is cautious and patient, while Uranus takes risks and is fast to act. Saturn is pragmatic and practical, while Uranus is progressive and impulsive. Saturn prefers traditional systems and follows established rules, but Uranus sees how things need to be improved and is always making up new rules. The question often facing Aquarians is: do I stick with what has worked up to now, or do I develop a new system? Many Aquarians are interested in the future and focused on bettering community outcomes.

Occupations like engineering are a good fit for the typical Aquarian. Engineers design and build systems and structures, so they need to be diligent and thorough. They solve problems using mathematics, science and technology. They are focused on improving future outcomes, but they are also patient and work through technical details step by step. Careers in social work, computer technology and community organisations also suit Aquarian types. Aquarians are idealists. Knowledge, freedom, independence, social justice and truth are all incredibly important. They are objective, principled and impartial and they are curious about the way things work.

In relationships, Aquarians are sociable and friendly, but sometimes appear cool and standoffish. Now and then they need their own space. Sometimes they display a complete lack of compassion. It can be difficult to get to know them. Overall, they tend to prefer intellectual companionship to long-term commitment. Many Aquarians opt for unconventional relationships and may even live in separate houses or in different states or countries to their partners. Often you will find Aquarians in relationships with other Aquarians because they understand one another.

Aquarius in Storytelling

Since Aquarius is associated with the planet Uranus, the future is important. Progress, technology and science are Aquarian areas of interest. In terms of genres associated with this sign, science fiction fits the bill.

Many science fiction stories are classic examples of the hero's journey, including modern-day movie franchises with their superheroes and amazing special effects. But this formula can become a little stale if the characters lack emotional depth. As heroes face the challenges of outer space, or some future or dystopian world, it's important to include a feeling of humanity and a meaningful message within the narrative.

Original books like HG Wells' *The Time Machine* (1895), which explores human evolution and societal structure, remain an example of thought-provoking work in the science fiction genre. Films like *Alien* (1979), *Blade Runner* (1982) and *The Matrix* (1999) are great examples of science fiction storytelling.

Other themes related to Aquarius are the characters who stand up to those in power and fight to change the system. James Dean's characters in *Rebel Without a Cause* (1955) and in *East of Eden* (1955) embody the essence of teenage rebellion.

Many stories are based on true events and the people who have fought to change the status quo. Based on historical events, in the movie *Braveheart* (1995), the rebel leader William Wallace (Mel Gibson) leads the Scottish resistance against English oppression. In another true story, the title character, *Erin Brockovich* (2000), is a legal assistant who takes on a powerful corporation accused of polluting a town's water supply. In the movie *Silkwood* (1983), Meryl Streep portrays Karen Silkwood, who blows the whistle on the dangerous activities at the nuclear facility where she worked.

These rebel characters serve as symbols of hope, courage and the willingness to challenge those in authority. Their stories inspire audiences and emphasise the power of the individual to make a difference, even in the face of seemingly insurmountable odds.

Well-known Aquarian Writers

Writers born with the Sun in Aquarius include Charles Dickens, Virginia Woolf, Lord Byron, Lewis Carroll and Jules Verne.

Pisces

Polarity: Yin

Quality: Mutable

Element: Water

Ruling Planets: Jupiter and Neptune

Symbol: The Fishes

Positive Traits: Compassionate, empathetic, imaginative. Receptive, charitable, intuitive.

Negative Traits: Vacillating, impressionable, escapist. Indecisive, depressive, deceptive.

The Symbolism of Pisces

Pisceans are instinctual beings who like to go with the flow. The combination of the mutable quality with the water element creates an ever-changing fluid atmosphere and a feeling that is difficult to define.

The symbol for Pisces is two fish with their tails tied together. They swim in opposite directions. Should I go with the flow? Or would it be better to swim upstream against the current? Sometimes fish seem to swim around in circles. Some fish swim in schools and others travel solo.

Pisceans are sensitive creatures who can experience psychic impressions and prophetic visions. With such an active imagination, Piscean possibilities are infinite, which is why it can be difficult for this sign to plan ahead and act decisively. Consequently, having a blueprint and a systematic approach can be enormously helpful.

A Pisces friend of mine works in a highly structured government department. She is in a senior position and a team leader. It's a complex organisation with a host of rules and systems that must be followed to the letter. The constraints of the organisation lead her to escape on holiday at every opportunity. She still enjoys visiting places where she can fully appreciate natural environments and allow her mind to unwind and her imagination to wander. True to her Piscean nature, she especially loves the water. It provides her with a vital escape.

Having form and structure in their lives is beneficial for Pisceans. Without it, the dreamy, fluid fish can just tread water forever. They can squirm and try to avoid capture and when hooked by reality, they will thrash about and try desperately to swim away, but deadlines and rules help Pisceans to turn their beautiful dreams and active imaginations into reality. Many people with Pisces emphasised in their birth charts have a great talent for music or art.

The harsh reality of the world can be difficult for Pisceans to face. They need to have a place to escape to. It may be a nature reserve, or an inner landscape of music, or art, or a deeper spiritual belief that sustains them; all are preferable to escaping reality by developing an alcohol or drug problem. Sadly, some Pisceans drown their sorrows and develop addictions. They can be prone to depression too.

Jupiter is the traditional ruling planet of Pisces and Neptune is its modern ruler. Both planets evoke a sense of expansiveness. Jupiter is the largest planet in our solar system and Neptune is a long way away, reflecting the vastness and universal scope associated with watery depths. Neptune is a deep and fluid symbol of infinite possibilities, where dreams and imagination flow freely. To Pisces, fairy tales and make-believe are just as real as sandcastles.

As far as Pisces is concerned, there's no right or wrong, no black or white. Everything is in shades of blue; all is connected; everything is included; nothing is separate or excluded. The last sign of the zodiac is acutely sensitive, a kind of psychic sponge, absorbing the moods and feelings of others, especially when people or animals are suffering. It's common to find Pisceans working in fields like social work, nursing, or mental health, where their compassion and understanding can be put to good use.

Pisceans can have trouble asserting themselves. They have broad awareness and understanding and a great deal of compassion, but they can lack a clear sense of self. Boundaries can become blurred and they can have difficulty saying no. Sometimes they neglect their own needs, or indeed can have trouble even comprehending that they have any needs. In providing help and assisting other people, they need to learn how to set limits to avoid losing their identity. As the last sign of the zodiac, Pisces is said to contain a little bit of all the other signs, which is why they have such universal awareness and empathy. Fish are the only creatures in the zodiac that live totally in a watery world and cannot breathe air. Other signs simply don't have the same depth of understanding.

Pisces in Storytelling

Piscean themes encompass genres that explore the psychic realm and romantic tales and fantasy stories, which allow the audience to escape into a magical world full of poetry, dreams and impressions.

There's an ocean full of stories involving fish and sea creatures. The mysterious depths of the ocean are explored in a host of watery tales. *The Little Mermaid* (1837) by Hans Christian Andersen is a fairy tale of a young mermaid who falls in love with a human prince. The story explores themes of sacrifice, love and the desire for a different life. In *The Fisherman and His Soul* by Oscar Wilde, we have another magical tale of a fisherman who falls in love with a mermaid.

Pisces themes are explored in the film *The Shape of Water* (2017), directed by Guillermo del Toro. In this fantasy romance film, the main human character, Elisa, cannot speak, but she forms a deep connection with a strange amphibious creature.

Another film, *What Lies Beneath* (2000), directed by Robert Zemeckis, is a supernatural thriller. The main character, Claire (Michelle Pfeiffer), has intensifying visions and becomes entangled in a ghostly mystery. Claire's visions guide her to a nearby lake where the woman's body is discovered.

Many classic myths and fairy tales evoke the watery feeling of Pisces and explore spiritual matters or mysterious happenings. Fantasy and magic, dream sequences and ghostly tales are all examples of the captivating and strangely hypnotic images that lure us into the depths of the imagination.

Well-known Pisces Writers

Writers born with the Sun in Pisces include Dr Seuss, Victor Hugo, John Steinbeck, Jack Kerouac and Douglas Adams.

2. CHARACTER AND PSYCHOLOGY

Each sign of the zodiac is a marriage of an element and a quality (also called mode, or modality). The four elements (fire, earth, air and water) combine with the three qualities (cardinal, fixed and mutable) to create the 12 signs of the zodiac. The elements and the qualities lie at the heart of astrological lore. These archetypes are so ingrained within people and in everyday life that we barely notice their presence. Understanding the fundamentals of the elements and qualities will provide you with deeper insight into human behaviour and relationships and guide your character development and story.

Polarity

Before we look at the elements and qualities, let's first consider polarity. Polarity is seen everywhere in pairs of opposites. Hot and cold, big and small, black and white, hard and soft, sweet and sour, wet and dry, male and female.

The astrological polarities were originally called masculine and feminine, or positive and negative, but there are other words we can use which avoid any gender bias or 'negative' associations. Yang and yin are the terms used in Eastern cultures to describe this essential pair of opposites. Extrovert and introvert are also a good way to describe these polarities.

All fire and air signs are yang or extroverted and all earth and water signs are yin or introverted. That doesn't mean that everyone born with the Sun in Aries is extroverted, nor are all people born with the Sun in Taurus introverted and so on. Always remember that the Sun in the birth chart is just one feature among many. Nevertheless, the signs themselves are classified as either yang or yin.

We all engage with people and the world, but the way we go about this differs. As a writer, when you are developing a character, it's important to understand their approach to life and their motivation. Are they driven by an inner feeling, a core set of values, a principle, or a conviction, or are they motivated by outer circumstances, a specific goal and other people?

Yang/Extrovert – Fire and Air
Aries, Gemini, Leo, Libra, Sagittarius, Aquarius.
- Outgoing and sociable
- Motivated by other people and external events
- Assertive and talkative
- Energetic and adventurous
- Can become despondent when they are alone
- Can become bored when there is not much going on
- Enjoy teamwork and group activities
- Want to have new and stimulating experiences

Yin/Introvert – Earth and Water

Taurus, Cancer, Virgo, Scorpio, Capricorn, Pisces.
- Inwardly focused and reserved
- Motivated from within by their inner convictions
- Formulate concepts internally through listening and observation
- Are content in their own company
- Focus on their work, hobbies and interests
- Can become overwhelmed when there is too much social interaction
- Need time alone to process events and retain their inner focus
- Want to deepen their understanding

In the zodiac, signs that are opposite one another have the same polarity, so while they are opposite in one sense, they still have something in common. Below are some of the intrinsic motivations of each sign and its opposing sign.

- Aries wants to lead others and be seen as independent and courageous.
- Libra wants to lead by engaging with others in a spirit of cooperation.

- Taurus is focused on establishing and maintaining core values and standards.
- Scorpio is focused on probing the deeper meaning behind life's mysteries.

- Gemini is interested in facilitating the exchange of ideas and information.
- Sagittarius is interested in exploring the world to seek truth and meaning.

- Cancer prioritises home and family to provide a feeling of security before proceeding.
- Capricorn prioritises duty and career to provide stability and security.

- Leo wants to express itself creatively to be a shining example to the world.
- Aquarius wants to engage with the community to create a better future for all.

- Virgo seeks to analyse and categorise life to create order and efficiency.
- Pisces seeks a meaningful connection with the universal source.

The Elements – Fire, Earth, Air, Water

The concept of the four elements (fire, earth, air and water) comes from early philosophical and alchemical traditions, which sought to understand and describe the fundamental building blocks of the physical world. Things that are elementary are archetypal, rudimentary, original and natural. Anything that is elementary is something basic from which more complex development can evolve. As Sherlock Holmes is often quoted as saying, 'It's elementary, my dear Watson,' although apparently this phrase never actually appeared in any of Arthur Conan Doyle's famous detective books.

Fire

The fire element is commonly associated with energy, courage and strength. It symbolises vitality and inspires action. Fire is warm, creative and enthusiastic. It's confident and outgoing. Taken to extremes, fire can become wild and destructive. Fire signs (Aries, Leo, Sagittarius) embody these characteristics. They are energetic, adventurous and optimistic.

Earth

Earth represents stability and grounding. It's the element of the material world. It symbolises the foundation upon which all things are built. The earth element is associated with the sustaining qualities of the natural world and with endurance. It's resilient, practical and realistic. Earth is stable, reliable and grounded. Earth signs (Taurus,

Virgo, Capricorn) are methodical and diligent. These signs have a strong sense of responsibility and a disciplined work ethic.

Air

Air represents the realm of thought, intellect and communication. It symbolises the mind, reasoning, logic and the exchange of ideas. Like the wind, air is linked to freedom and mobility and represents the capacity for human interaction. Air signs are intellectual and rational and they make decisions based on reason and logic. The air signs (Gemini, Libra and Aquarius) are curious, sociable and impartial.

Water

Water represents the realm of emotions, feelings, imagination and intuition. Water is fluid and adaptable and takes the shape of its container. In terms of personality, individuals associated with the water element are emotional, empathetic and sensitive and they make decisions based on their feelings. Water signs (Cancer, Scorpio, Pisces) are imaginative and compassionate.

The Humours

The concept of the four humours, known as humourism, is an ancient theory dating back to the time of Hippocrates in Greece. It was based on the belief that human health and personality were determined by the balance of four humours.

Each humour is associated with one of the four classical elements:
- The choleric temperament is associated with fire. This type was forthright, outgoing, assertive and competitive.
- The melancholy temperament is associated with earth. This individual was introspective, practical, focused and patient.
- The sanguine temperament is associated with air. A sanguine individual was cheerful, optimistic, extroverted and sociable.
- The phlegmatic temperament is associated with water. This type was calm, sensitive, thoughtful and empathetic.

Humourism was an accepted theory in medicine for around two thousand years. It was thought that physical illness and personality disorders were caused by an imbalance of the humours and various treatments were prescribed to restore equilibrium.

Jung's Psychological Types

The Swiss psychologist Carl Jung presented his own analysis of these four categories of temperament and personality. In his work *Psychological Types,* Jung named them intuition, sensation, thinking, and feeling. They are virtually identical to the elements fire, earth, air and water. Astrologer and Jungian analyst Liz Greene explored the natural affinity between the four astrological elements and Jung's psychological types in her wonderful book, *Relating: An Astrological Guide to Living with Others on a Small Planet*, first published in 1978.

In Jung's system, intuition (fire) and sensation (earth) are mutually exclusive, psychologically speaking. They are both methods of perception. Intuition (fire) is interested in future potential, the purpose of things and how things might develop. Intuition (fire) tends to see things in broad terms. In essence, it's right-brained and focused on the big picture of possibilities. By contrast, sensation (earth) sees things in more detail, is left-brained, practical and hands-on. Sensation (earth) perceives the world and its surroundings just as they are and focuses on the practical way things can be used in the here-and-now. Whichever of these two psychological types is conscious and therefore dominant, the other is mostly unconscious. Consequently, the unconscious element/type is often projected onto others.

Similarly, thinking (air) and feeling (water) are mutually exclusive. These are methods of evaluating our experiences. People tend to be more conscious of one element/type and disown and project the other. Thinking (air) assesses experiences rationally, logically and without personal bias. It places more value on science, theories and principles than on personal experience. Alternatively, feeling (water) evaluates experiences subjectively according to their personal worth and intrinsic meaningfulness.

To summarise:
- Intuition (fire) and thinking (air) are more extroverted.
- Sensation (earth) and feeling (water) are more introverted.
- Intuition (fire) and feeling (water) are more right-brained.
- Sensation (earth) and thinking (air) are more left-brained.

You might be familiar with the Myers-Briggs Type Indicator (MBTI). Developed by Katharine Cook Briggs and her daughter, Isabel Briggs Myers, and based on Jung's psychological types. This psychological test describes 16 personality types and is used extensively in the business sector to provide psychological assessments of employees and in a wide range of other settings.

Later, David Keirsey used the MBTI to develop the Keirsey Temperament Sorter and gave each of the 16 types a specific name, such as Inspector (ISTJ), Counsellor (INFJ), Performer (ESFP), Teacher (ENFJ) and so on.

To gain further insight into human behaviour you may wish to delve deeper into Jungian psychology, but a good grounding in astrology will give you the keys to develop meaningful characters and understand their motivation and personal preferences, as well as their psychological blind spots and personal challenges.

Whichever system you examine, the humours, the elements, Jung's psychological types, or Keirsey, this organic four-fold system is a fundamental component of human personality.

Elemental Correspondences

	Fire	Earth	Air	Water
Humours	Choleric	Melancholic	Sanguine	Phlegmatic
Jung	Intuition	Sensation	Thinking	Feeling
Keirsey	Artisan	Guardian	Rationalist	Idealist
Traits	Confident	Diligent	Friendly	Receptive
	Spontaneous	Methodical	Rational	Caring
	Passionate	Sensible	Idealistic	Sensitive
	Active	Practical	Sceptical	Compassionate
	Creative	Reliable	Scientific	Emotional
	Outgoing	Reserved	Sociable	Nurturing
	Expressive	Conservative	Detached	Imaginative

In developing your characters, bear in mind that one element/type is usually underdeveloped. As a result, the individual concerned will often struggle when they run into characters and situations that embody their unconscious element. For example, in the popular TV series *The Tunnel,* the female detective, Elise Wassermann, is a classic thinking type (air) while her colleague, Karl Roebuck, is a feeling type (water). She is straightforward and very direct in her manner and has the same businesslike attitude towards her sex partners. Karl chastises her for being unsympathetic towards witnesses. Somehow, they must work out how to cooperate despite their differences.

When you look, it's easy to see examples of the four classic elements/types in film and television. Characters who personify the elements are familiar and memorable. Whether consciously or unconsciously, many writers have drawn upon the four elements to create relatable and believable characters. Let's look at a few examples.

The Wizard of Oz

The classic 1939 movie *The Wizard of Oz* is based on a book by L. Frank Baum, *The Wonderful Wizard of Oz*, published in 1900. Baum wrote 14 novels in the Oz series. He also wrote more than 40 other novels, over 80 short stories, 42 scripts, plus more than 200 poems.

The Wizard of Oz features four main characters, each of whom is a clear representation of the elements. Dorothy symbolises the earth element. She lives on a farm with her uncle and aunt and her dog, Toto. Toto bites the grumpy Miss Gulch, who obtains an order for Toto to be put down. Dorothy and Toto run away and are swept up into a tornado, which takes them to a strange and unfamiliar place. Dorothy starts out on a journey along the yellow brick road to find the Wizard who can help her get home to Kansas. She wants to return to the security and stability of the earth.

Dorothy meets the Scarecrow, who symbolises the air element and the thinking function. All he wants is a brain. She encounters the Tin Man, symbolising the water element and feeling function, for all he wants is a heart. Then Dorothy meets the Cowardly Lion, a representation of the fire element and intuitive function, as he is seeking courage.

The four of them set off to find the Wizard, who they believe will solve all their problems. As the story unfolds, Dorothy and her companions face various obstacles and tests. Along the way, the Scarecrow learns that he always had a brain, the Tin Man discovers he has a heart and the Lion becomes courageous.

In their quest to find the Wizard, they discover the aspects of character they thought they were lacking. The Wizard is just an ordinary man, without any special powers. The four main characters have done all the work themselves and become conscious of the attributes they never knew they possessed. All the while, Dorothy has had the protection of her ruby red slippers symbolising her connection to the earth. All she has to do is click her heels together to arrive safely back home.

Gone With the Wind

The four main characters in the classic 1939 movie *Gone with the Wind*, based on the book by Margaret Mitchell, are another example of the personification of the elements. These characters have layers of complexity. They are not just one type, but each character is an amalgam of types.

Scarlett O'Hara is primarily of the fire element. Her very name, Scarlett, is an apt description of her fiery and passionate nature. She's headstrong and wilful, vain and self-centred. Through all her trials, she's independent and follows her heart no matter what. But she's also materialistic and has an earthy, practical side to her. The red earth of Tara is where she gets her strength and resilience, but in the beginning, she does not realise this. After the destruction wrought by the Civil War, Scarlett becomes obsessed with making money. She swears that she will do anything and everything, lie, cheat or steal so that she will never go hungry again. Her character is therefore an interesting mix of fire and earth, which are elements/types that are contradictory. She also has air in her nature. She's practical and matter-of-fact and follows her own ideas. The only element she truly lacks is water. She turns on the tears when it suits her. She has no compassion for others, no real empathy and is completely insensitive.

Rhett Butler is associated with the earth element as he is well-to-do, focused on material wealth and provides practical assistance when called upon. But he's more extroverted, passionate and chivalrous than the classic earthy type. He comes to the rescue when Scarlett is in need and on several occasions he also helps Melanie. Like the Earth element, he is resourceful, but he is also fiery and passionate, and has some air too. He engages in social relationships with Belle Watling and her girls and, in one scene, takes part in a friendly game of cards, gambling with the officers who have arrested him. Like Scarlett, Rhett also lacks water, but over time his character develops compassion and understanding, which is expressed in his respect for Melanie and in his love for his daughter, Bonnie. Scarlett, however, remains devoid of feeling.

Interestingly, both Scarlett and Rhett are mostly a blend of two opposing types, fire and earth, or intuition and sensation, to use the Jungian terms. In one another, they recognise these aspects of themselves and acknowledge their similarities. The fiery, passionate nature of their relationship takes many twists and turns. At first Scarlett is indifferent to Rhett's advances, then she enjoys his attention and his wealth, then she hates him while still enjoying the lavish lifestyle he provides. Her opinion of him is constantly changing. Scarlett is always professing her love for Ashley.

The relationship between Scarlett and Rhett deteriorates and implodes. When Melanie dies, Scarlett realises she really loves Rhett and never really loved Ashley. She heads off through the fog to reconcile with Rhett. But Rhett has had enough of her torment and leaves. After all the pain and misery that Scarlett and Rhett have inflicted on one another, will they ever be able to salvage their marriage? The eternal optimist, Scarlett, vows to win him back.

Ashley Wilkes represents the air element. He is an idealist, but he's more introverted than the typical air type. His tendency to theorise about the political situation and detach himself emotionally from all that is happening around him is typical of air. He's a bit earthy too, rather pragmatic about his choice of Melanie as a wife, because he says they are alike. He's also watery, with a tendency to go with the flow. Ashley is a rather remote figure who admires Scarlett for her fire and energy, which are the qualities he lacks. He loves her enthusiasm and passion. Just as Scarlett lacks water, Ashley lacks fire. But the water that Scarlett is seeking isn't that deep in Ashley. He's in denial of his feelings. He has made a pragmatic and socially acceptable choice in his wife, Melanie. Ashley and Melanie are alike too. Both characters lack fire. All the while Scarlett professes her love for Ashley, she is projecting onto him the element she lacks (water). Since Ashley lacks fire, he is attracted to Scarlett, but Ashley obeys the laws of society and values the principles of duty and honour above all.

Melanie Wilkes is a clear example of the water element. She's caring, gentle and compassionate. She always puts the needs of others before her own. She only has good things to say about everyone, including Scarlett, despite the fact that Scarlett sees Melanie as weak and treats her with contempt. Melanie even forgives Scarlett when Scarlett is discovered kissing her husband, Ashley. Like her husband, Melanie lacks fire and therefore she admires Scarlett.

The Golden Girls

Created by prolific television writer Susan Harris, *The Golden Girls* sitcom ran for seven seasons from 1985 to 1992. The comedy features four older women, three widows and one divorcee, who share a house in Florida. The show won several Golden Globes and Emmy awards and each of the actors also won Emmys.

Dorothy is the central character in this sitcom and like *The Wizard of Oz*, this Dorothy is also associated with the earth element. Played by Bea Arthur, with her characteristically deep voice, Dorothy is practical and down-to-earth. Her manner is dead-pan and she's always pointing out obvious facts.

Her mother Sophia, played by Estelle Getty, is a classic air type, rational and quick-witted. She speaks her mind. Sophia was born in Sicily and she often tells stories about her early life. She says things like, 'In Sicily it was good luck to bury someone you hate' and 'If you wanted to impress someone in Sicily, you shot their brother.'

The fiery, passionate one is Blanche (Rue McClanahan) who is self-centred, vain and an exhibitionist. Blanche is promiscuous and is always going out on a date with a new man. She wears extravagant clothes and bright colours.

The fourth member of the group is Rose (Betty White) who is a classic water type, caring, sensitive, naive and vague. In the beginning of the series, Rose works as a counsellor, which is a typical occupation for a water type. To the annoyance of the other characters, she often tells long stories about growing up in St Olaf, Minnesota, a small community where the people were simple.

These characters are caricatures, exaggerated examples of the four elements, which is why they are funny. In real life, an element rarely manifests in such exaggerated manner in one individual. But these four characters are true to life, in the sense that they are archetypal and therefore relatable.

Sex and the City

We see the same four-fold character structure in the sitcom *Sex and the City*, based on the book of the same name written by Candace Bushnell. It ran from 1998 to 2004 with the four main characters symbolising each of the four elements.

Carrie Bradshaw is the main protagonist. She represents the water element. She is looking for emotional security and a steady relationship. She is the narrator and writes a freelance column about sex and relationships. When she is faced with eviction, Carrie comes to realise how much she values the security of her rented apartment. Carrie must face up to her habit of spending all her income on shoes and borrows money from Charlotte so she can buy her apartment.

Charlotte York represents the earth element. She is materially secure and conservative in her views. Charlotte comes from a wealthy family and does not need to work, but she enjoys her job as an art dealer. She is seeking a traditional relationship. She is often critical of Samantha's sexual antics, but despite her conservative views, Charlotte occasionally and secretly dabbles in some sexual escapades of her own.

Samantha Jones is clearly the feisty and passionate fire element. A publicity-hungry exhibitionist, she works in public relations. She's confident and honest and enjoys being single. She values her independence and goes out of her way to avoid being pinned down by a permanent relationship. She avoids any kind of emotional connection, but over the course of her journey, we learn that she does have a heart.

Miranda Hobbes represents the air element. She values her independence and doesn't want to become emotionally involved.

She is a lawyer with a strong career drive and not at all interested in marriage. She's rather cynical about relationships. When she falls pregnant, she decides to raise her child on her own, but eventually she settles down with her partner Steve, and her son Brady.

Each of the characters must come to terms with qualities that they lack. Carrie lacks the practicality of earth. Charlotte lacks the extroversion of fire. Both Samantha and Miranda lack the emotions and feeling nature of the water element.

Seinfeld

We again see the four elements personified in the central characters in the popular '90s sitcom *Seinfeld*, created by Larry David and Jerry Seinfeld. It screened for nine seasons from 1989 to 1998.

The central character, Jerry, is earthy and practical. He has been described as 'the voice of reason'. The antics of his eccentric neighbour, Kramer, who represents the fire element, often disrupt his orderly life. Fire is spontaneous and it can be wild. Jerry is often trying to bring some order and structure to Kramer's life, to no avail. Kramer often tries to get Jerry to try new and exciting things, with limited success.

Elaine represents air (thinking). She is unemotional, career focused and straightforward. She and Jerry used to be in a relationship and after their break-up, they remain friends. Earth and air share a no-nonsense, left-brain perspective, so they have a lot in common.

George is paranoid and insecure. Often unemployed, he still lives with his parents. He's a pessimist and is often depressed. George is the water element, the psychological opposite of air. Elaine often teases him about his insecurities.

In a trailer promoting the release of the series on Netflix, earthy Jerry is described as 'neurotic', just like the pedantic earth element. George is classified as 'the coward', a negative attribute of water. Elaine is called 'the cynic', which is typical of the element air and Kramer is called 'the wild card' in keeping with the fire element when it gets out of hand.

Fawlty Towers

This often repeated, hilarious British sitcom first aired in the 1970s. Set in a fictional hotel in the seaside town of Torquay, England, the show revolves around the chaotic situations which arise from the interactions of the hotel's eccentric and dysfunctional staff and guests. Like the *Golden Girls*, these characters have exaggerated traits based on the four elements. They are caricatures, making for great comedy.

Basil Fawlty (John Cleese) is the perpetually stressed-out owner of Fawlty Towers. He is rude to his guests and has a short temper. Basil tries to control the chaos that swirls around him, but he is the one who creates the most chaos. He is like a wildfire, totally out of control. He lacks the earth element, so he has difficulty managing the day-to-day running of the hotel. Basil has no skills in managing practical matters, such as repairs.

Sybil Fawlty (Prunella Scales) is Basil's long-suffering wife, who manages the hotel alongside him. She is level-headed, practical and patient, qualities consistent with the earth element. Sybil tries her best to keep things organised, but her efforts are often in vain. Sybil and Basil are psychological opposites.

Manuel (Andrew Sachs) is the well-meaning but bumbling Spanish waiter from Barcelona. He struggles with the English language, leading to hilarious misunderstandings and confusion. Manuel is associated with the water element. He tries his best to please.

Polly Sherman (Connie Booth) is the competent and sensible housemaid at Fawlty Towers who often has to pick up the pieces of the chaos surrounding her. She's intelligent and capable, which are qualities associated with the air element.

Suits

The outstanding television series *Suits* also features these four archetypal characters. This successful legal drama ran for nine seasons from 2011 through 2019. It was created by Aaron Korsh.

Mike Ross is a brilliant law student with a photographic memory, but he's expelled from university and never completes his studies. Mike's parents were killed in a car accident when he was 11 years old and he was raised by his grandmother. Mike tries to make money to support his grandmother by doing shady drug deals for his mate, Trevor. In the process he stumbles into a job interview with Harvey Specter, who is recruiting Harvard graduates for his law firm, Pearson Hardman. Harvey is so impressed by Mike's quick thinking and his vast legal knowledge, he hires him on the spot, despite knowing that Mike is unqualified and unlicensed to practice law. Mike is the fire element. He's a wild card, highly creative, spontaneous and brilliant.

Harvey Specter represents the air element. He's capable and deals with a host of legal problems, winning cases, settling them and getting results. Harvey is principled up to a point but believes the ends justify the means. He will bend the law in order to win. Harvey relies on his intuitive secretary, Donna, who knows immediately that Harvey has hired Mike illegally. Donna is in love with Harvey and he is in love with her, but he is in denial of his feelings because he does not want to be distracted from his work. But we discover his emotional issues go deeper.

Eventually, managing partner, Jessica Pearson, finds out Mike's secret and what Harvey has done. She's outraged, but she realises she must accept the situation because now she, Harvey and the firm, are in breach of the law. Mike is also doing wonderful work for the firm's clients. Jessica is pragmatic and represents the earth element. She's focused on managing her law firm to ensure its financial success. She deals with a host of day-to-day issues and tries to keep things on an even keel. Her business responsibilities always take precedence over her personal happiness.

Louis Litt is the water element in the mix. He's emotional, sensitive and neurotic. The other characters try desperately to keep Mike's secret hidden from Louis, knowing that he won't handle it well and will probably spill the beans, exposing Mike and the firm to the authorities. Louis thinks of his colleagues as family. When Louis finds out about Mike's secret, he feels betrayed by everyone.

Just as fire (intuition) and earth (sensation) are opposing functions, Mike and Jessica are in conflict. She was forced to accept Mike into the firm and she resents his presence. There is even more conflict and tension between Harvey (air/thinking) and Louis (feeling/water). They are always at loggerheads.

Meanwhile, Donna who is a highly intuitive character, understands everyone and everything. She often tries to convey to Harvey how his unfeeling actions hurt Louis. Donna is always one step ahead and acts as a mediator between the other characters who often confide in her. Even when they don't, she knows what they are feeling and what is going on. In a way, she is an amalgam of all the elements.

Each of the characters has issues from their past which affect their relationships with one another. The show explores how their experiences have shaped them. The whole nine seasons, 134 episodes, run for over 90 hours. It showcases outstanding character development and explores the complexity of relationships. The show includes wonderfully scripted storylines and fantastic dialogue.

Archetypal Characters

	Fire	Earth	Air	Water
Golden Girls	Blanche	Dorothy	Sophia	Rose
Wizard of Oz	Lion	Dorothy	Scarecrow	Tin Man
Sex and the City	Samantha	Charlotte	Miranda	Carrie
Seinfeld	Kramer	Jerry	Elaine	George
Gone with the Wind	Scarlet	Rhett	Ashley	Melanie
Fawlty Towers	Basil	Sybil	Polly	Manuel
Suits	Mike	Jessica	Harvey	Louis

The Qualities – Cardinal, Fixed, Mutable

The three qualities, which are also called modes or modalities, are another fundamental division of the zodiac. Signs of the same quality are square, or opposite one another. Because they are 90 or 180 degrees apart, signs of the same quality are in a state of tension and potential conflict with one another. If you want to create drama in your narrative, one of the best ways to do this is to learn about the modalities.

The qualities correspond with the annual cycle of the seasons. Each season on Earth begins when the Sun enters one of the four cardinal signs, Aries, Cancer, Libra and Capricorn. The second month of each season brings the most concentrated energy and weather conditions when the Sun is in fixed signs, Taurus, Leo, Scorpio and Aquarius. During the third month of each season, the Sun is moving through mutable signs, Gemini, Virgo, Sagittarius and Pisces when the weather is changeable. These seasonal cycles mirror the intrinsic characteristics of each zodiac sign.

Cardinal Signs – Aries, Cancer, Libra, Capricorn

The word 'cardinal' means, chief, pivotal, or essential. Interestingly, it also means, 'pertaining to a hinge'. Events hinge on these moments, so each cardinal sign is a key turning point, or threshold crossing. Cardinal signs are associated with decision making and committing to a course of action. The cardinal signs are so called because the Sun enters these signs at key moments in Earth's orbit, at the equinoxes and the solstices.

These points in space-time are significant markers in our annual journey, so the four cardinal signs are associated with key areas of life. Aries is about self-expression and independence. Cancer's realm is home and family. Libra's focus is on relationships. Capricorn concerns itself with goals and career and our standing in the world. These are the chief priorities of the cardinal signs.

The four cardinal signs are known for their initiative and for taking charge. These signs are naturally ambitious and driven and they enjoy starting and leading new projects. Cardinal signs are self-motivated, enterprising and assertive.

When two or more people want to take charge and make the decisions, this will naturally create a situation where there will be conflict. What path should we follow? Who ends up being the leader and who must give way? This tension can also exist within one individual. For example, your protagonist might be torn between two courses of action.

Because of their primary position, cardinal signs are excellent self-starters, but they can over-commit. Consequently, they can run into trouble when trying to complete tasks. They like to start projects and lead them, but sometimes they can have difficulty following through because they have taken on too much. Staying power is where the fixed signs come into their own.

Fixed Signs – Taurus, Leo, Scorpio, Aquarius

While the summer solstice marks the start of summer, this is not the hottest time of the year. Planet Earth is just like your kitchen oven, after you switch it on, it takes a while to heat up. When you turn your oven off, just like at the winter solstice, it takes a while to cool down.

The most extreme temperatures on Earth happen when the Sun is in the fixed signs of Leo and Aquarius. These climatic extremes take place around the first week of February and the first week of August. This is when the Sun is halfway between the solstices and equinoxes and therefore in the middle of these fixed signs. When the Sun is in the other two fixed signs, Taurus and Scorpio, we experience the full flowering of spring and the time of the year when leaves drop from trees, life retreats underground and hibernation starts in autumn/fall.

The four fixed signs are known for their stability, persistence and endurance. They are determined, loyal and passionate and they don't give up easily. They're highly resistant to change. If people are unwilling to give ground and are determined to maintain their position, this too will create situations where there is conflict. If your main protagonist has a lot of fixed energy, their personality will trigger tension, which can drive your story, especially when they encounter other characters and situations that are equally rigid. When neither party is willing to give way and refuses to negotiate or compromise, you are sure to end up with a tense stand-off.

While cardinal signs initiate proceedings, fixed signs make sure that tasks are completed. Fixed signs get results. They never give up and have immense willpower. They use their mental and emotional strength to fight for what they believe in. Once they set themselves a task, they stick with it until the bitter end. When fixed signs encounter one another, fixed feuds and stalemates can occur.

Their determination and rigidity make it challenging for fixed signs to adjust to change. They can become inflexible and stubborn. Circumstances have a habit of changing, but fixed signs prefer to stick with the status quo. It's the mutable signs that cope best with change.

Mutable Signs – Gemini, Virgo, Sagittarius, Pisces

The Sun is located in mutable signs when the weather is changing and we are in between seasons. At these times of the year, there are often a lot of fluctuations in temperature and other weather variables, which makes it difficult to know what to expect. Sudden weather events can catch us off guard. Have I worn the right clothes for the conditions? Should I carry an umbrella? One day it can be warm, the next freezing cold and it can be windy, as hot and cold air currents fight one another for dominance.

When something unexpected happens, fixed signs can find it hard to cope, but mutable signs take it in their stride. Mutable signs are adaptable. They are accustomed to dealing with a variety of conditions. Gemini and Virgo are both ruled by fast-moving Mercury. These two signs are adept at managing an endless array of information and details. They are excellent communicators. Sagittarius and Pisces are traditionally ruled by Jupiter, whose expansiveness and broad perspective provide these signs with the vision to see ahead. Pisces can also explore infinite possibilities thanks to Neptune, its modern ruler. When things change, or when multiple options are present, mutable signs excel at managing these scenarios. They easily adapt to unforeseen circumstances.

The four mutable signs are known for their adaptability and flexibility. They go with the flow and adjust to change easily. They are versatile, can multitask and have a variety of interests. But when mutable signs interact, chaotic situations can develop. When there is constant change and no stability or direction, random events generate uncertainty. When an excess of mutable energy is present in one individual, they can arouse a constant state of flux and confusion.

Because mutable signs are so versatile, they sometimes have difficulty making firm commitments. Unlike the cardinal signs, leadership is not their strong suit. Nor are they especially good at following through like the fixed signs. In fact, when there is too much of the same routine, even Virgo, who thanks to the earth element is probably the most stable and grounded of the mutable signs, can become bored and stale when there is not enough variety on offer. Taken to extremes, mutable signs can be very restless, constantly jumping from one thing to another. They can become easily distracted.

The word 'mutable' stems from the root 'mei', which means to change, or to move. Associated words that come from this root include: communicate, emigrate, mistake, municipal, mutant, permeable, remunerate and transmute.

When mutable signs interact, forming oppositions, or square aspects, things can become very confusing. Communication problems and misunderstandings can quickly multiply, leading to chaos.

Zodiac Sign Summary

Sign	Element	Quality	Ruling Planet/s
Aries	Fire	Cardinal	Mars
Taurus	Earth	Fixed	Venus
Gemini	Air	Mutable	Mercury
Cancer	Water	Cardinal	Moon
Leo	Fire	Fixed	Sun
Virgo	Earth	Mutable	Mercury
Libra	Air	Cardinal	Venus
Scorpio	Water	Fixed	Pluto (Mars)
Sagittarius	Fire	Mutable	Jupiter
Capricorn	Earth	Cardinal	Saturn
Aquarius	Air	Fixed	Uranus (Saturn)
Pisces	Water	Mutable	Neptune (Jupiter)

Use this table to become more familiar with the essential components of each sign. As you construct your story and characters, review the elements, qualities, the signs and their ruling planets.

3. RELATIONSHIPS AND CONFLICT

People are not just one sign, but a mix of signs. There are a lot of planets in the solar system and a map of the heavens when we are born symbolises the various themes, values and perspectives of the individual. The challenges and obstacles we encounter in life provide opportunities for personal development. These tests help to raise consciousness. And so it is in storytelling.

The angular relationships between the planets and the signs are called aspects. Aspects are determined by dividing the 360 degrees of the zodiac into segments. When a planet in one sign aspects another planet in another sign, it tells us how the two get along with one another. Do they see eye to eye? Do they offer support to one other, or are they in competition or conflict? Each sign of the zodiac has a relationship to all the other signs. Some of these relationships are harmonious and others are challenging.

By understanding aspects, you can develop characters who have inner conflicts, write stories driven by characters' interactions and create events that challenge your main protagonist. Conflict drives stories because readers want to find out what happens next. How does your hero manage the problem? Do they overcome their difficulties? How are they changed by events? Is there an inner conflict within the psyche of your main character? Is this deeper issue resolved?

Challenging hard aspects (squares and oppositions) can generate:
- **Inner conflict.** Your protagonist has a psychological problem. This might stem from an event in their past, such as a traumatic incident, or a struggle they faced in childhood.
- **Relationship conflict.** Your protagonist is involved in a tense relationship with someone who has challenging characteristics. Your character might learn something through engaging with this person, leading to personal development.
- **Events conflict.** Your protagonist experiences a significant event that transforms their ordinary world. Events can shed light on how the past has led them to the present and the person they are.

Helpful easy aspects (sextiles and trines) describe:
- A helper or sidekick comes along at just the right time to offer useful advice and support to your hero/heroine.
- Your protagonist receives advice from a mentor or teacher whom they respect for their wisdom.

Tricky, uncertain aspects (semi-sextiles and quincunxes) deliver:
- A trickster or unexpected event which creates uncertainty.
- A surprise with unforeseen consequences.
- There is something mysterious going on, but your hero is unaware of what is happening.

Conjunctions

Matching signs: The same polarity, the same element, the same quality.

As you might imagine, there is a lot of common ground between people who have planets in the same sign. While every individual has unique characteristics, when two people have an abundance of planets in the same sign, they will most likely see eye to eye on most subjects. Relationships between two people of the same sign are usually comfortable and develop easily. They are kindred spirits. They look at life from the same perspective, often sharing the same opinions, the same values and general approach to life.

Even so, issues can develop in any relationship. While conjunctions are close connections, these relationships don't tend to foster personal growth. We can all fall into patterns and life can become predictable. When this happens in relationships, we can start to take others for granted, or we might feel like we are being ignored or undervalued. This can be the case with matching signs.

Another area of concern is that these signs share the same quality, which can lead to difficulties. With conjunctions in the cardinal signs (Aries, Cancer, Libra or Capricorn), we can easily fall into the pattern where one person is always making the decisions, which can lead to feelings of resentment by the other individual. Two people of the same fixed sign (Taurus, Leo, Scorpio or Aquarius) can end up at loggerheads. A tense stand-off or battle can ensue because neither person is willing to give way. With mutable sign conjunctions (in Gemini, Virgo, Sagittarius or Pisces) partners can enjoy one another's company, but the danger here is that there is too much change and instability to sustain a long-term connection.

Conjunctions can play out in other ways, by creating too much emphasis in one sign. For example, with fire signs (Aries, Leo or

Sagittarius) relationships can become competitive as each person tries to outshine the other. If the two people are the same earth sign (Taurus, Virgo or Capricorn) the relationship is usually stable, but over time it can become routine, dull and boring. With an air sign conjunction (Gemini, Libra or Aquarius) there is always a lot of social engagement outside the relationship, so other people can influence and interfere with the core of the relationship, leading to a feeling of distance and disconnection. With water signs (Cancer, Scorpio or Pisces) the depth of understanding brings a feeling of emotional support, but if one person is always more needy than the other, issues around give and take can arise.

Overall, conjunctions foster a feeling of connection and security. But regardless of how close and supportive the association, there are always going to be points of difference between people. With matching signs, these differences are among the easier ones to manage.

In storytelling, you can associate the conjunction with your hero's ordinary world. It's familiar, comfortable and secure. It's the starting point of any journey and it's also the end of the story, the ultimate destination. From the outset, your protagonist must commit to a journey, or nothing will change. Otherwise, there is no story; there are no events, no relationships and no personal growth. Nothing is going to happen if things just stay as they are. Like Dorothy in the *Wizard of Oz*, the ultimate destination might be to get back home again, but along the way the experiences we have and the people we meet will affect us and change us, just as we will influence others. In the process, we are transformed.

Semi-sextiles

Unfamiliar signs: Different polarity, different element, different quality.

Signs that are adjacent to one another have neither polarity, nor element, nor quality in common. Even so, they are close to one another because they share a cusp. They are like our next-door neighbours. Just like the people who live next door, it's a good idea to establish a friendly relationship with our neighbouring signs, but this relationship is only happening because we are in close proximity. We don't have anything in common and we really have no idea what these people are like, what their interests might be, what their political views are, or indeed what's going on behind closed doors. Just like our real-life neighbours, these characters might be passionate about keeping the house clean, or they might be hoarders with piles of junk stacked up to the rafters. Whatever their situation or interests, we really have no idea what makes them tick.

There are a couple of ways that adjacent signs interact, which can be useful in storytelling. Because zodiac signs are placed in a particular order, whatever sign/archetype informs your main character, the sign before can describe their back story. It's what your protagonist has already experienced. For example, if your main character is most like a Gemini, they have already established a firm set of values from the sign before (Taurus) and what they are lacking now is associated with the following sign, which they will meet in the future, in this example, Cancer. Geminis live in their heads, not their hearts and so while they are busy social networking, their real journey is often about getting in touch with their feelings and learning to understand and value emotional intelligence and not just sharing information, or giving their opinion.

The sign ahead in time is the future and the future is unknown. It's where we are heading, the path we are going to take. But like the hero who is called to adventure, the first step is often tentative. We really have no idea what we will encounter. One thing is clear: we are venturing into the unknown.

Semi-sextile relationships take us out of our comfort zone. Each sign can learn a great deal from the following sign and teach something to the sign before. Sometimes though, we are unwilling to move forward. Fear of the future and fear of the unknown are common emotions and humans are also very good at denial. Maybe if we ignore the problem, it will go away. People are content to stick with the devil they know. When we get advice from someone who has already experienced what we are going through, we are often reluctant to listen.

A good example of this relationship is the marriage of Queen Elizabeth II and Prince Phillip. She was a Taurus; he was a Gemini. As depicted in the TV series *The Crown*, Phillip was a curious man interested in new ideas. This is typical of mutable air. Elizabeth was a Taurus, the sign before Gemini. As a fixed earth sign, she was comfortable with the status quo. In season five of *The Crown*, the tension in their relationship escalates. Prince Phillip tries to encourage his wife to open her mind and try new things, but she is resistant to change. During her long reign, the Queen fulfilled her duty and adhered to the traditions of the British monarchy. She was reluctant to modernise and struggled to adapt.

The semi-sextile aspect speaks to these scenarios and it can be used to develop a range of situations where your protagonist encounters something foreign or strange that they are compelled to face, though they are unwilling to do so.

Aries is assertive, impulsive and heroic, but lacks the patience of Taurus.

Taurus is patient, determined and thorough, but lacks the versatility of Gemini.

Gemini is versatile, quick-witted and sociable, but lacks the emotional depth of Cancer.

Cancer is receptive, expressive and caring, but lacks the self-confidence of Leo.

Leo is confident, proud and dramatic, but lacks Virgo's ability to focus on details.

Virgo is analytical, self-sufficient and precise, but lacks Libra's relationship skills.

Libra is good at relationships, is fair and just, but lacks Scorpio's emotional depth.

Scorpio is deep, intense and resourceful, but lacks the faith and trust of Sagittarius.

Sagittarius is outgoing, open and trusting, but lacks the self-discipline of Capricorn.

Capricorn is disciplined, reliable and conventional, but lacks Aquarian spontaneity.

Aquarius is spontaneous, progressive and knowledgeable, but lacks Piscean empathy.

Pisces is empathetic, imaginative and impressionable, but lacks the self-belief of Aries.

Sextiles

Complementary signs: The same polarity, compatible element, different quality.

Sextile relationships are arguably the best combination for any relationship. Whether friends, colleagues, family members, partners or lovers, signs that are 60 degrees apart support one another. The sextile is a harmonious aspect, linking signs that have complimentary elements. Be it fire and air, or earth and water, both these combinations are highly compatible. Unlike the trine, which links signs of the same element, the sextile provides both a sense of security and adds a bit of spice. We're usually eager to engage with those who are two signs away from us. We often feel generous towards them.

The sextile aspect has an air-like feel to it. Two signs away from the starting point of the zodiac, 0 Aries, we are in Aquarius and Gemini territory, which are both air signs. This means that any two signs that are 60 degrees apart can communicate with one another easily and engage with each other in a friendly and sociable way. As we know, good communication is a key component in all relationships.

Earth signs offer structure and stability to water signs who enjoy the feeling of security that earth signs provide. Water signs help earth signs to engage more with their feelings. Earth signs feel nourished by the presence of water. As a result, both signs become more secure and productive.

Air signs encourage fire signs to share their creative gifts with others and build a network to support their expression, plus air helps fire develop some left-brain practicality. Fire signs help air signs to become more creative and warm-hearted, developing their right-brain and learning to value intuition.

In storytelling, sidekicks and helpers evoke the energy of the sextile relationship. These characters offer support and guidance to your main protagonist. Helpers often appear in stories after the hero has been called to adventure and is preparing for the journey they will undertake. Someone comes along who encourages your hero to keep going. They stand by your hero and provide the necessary tools or information.

Squares

Conflicting signs: Different polarity, different element, the same quality.

Squares create tension. They are the most challenging of all aspects. They are complex and fraught with conflict. Though squares are inherently difficult, they are catalysts for personal development and productivity.

One of the signs in a square aspect is yang (extrovert) and the other is yin (introvert). While one sign wants to go out and engage with others socially, the other prefers to stay home and devote time to their hobbies and personal interests. Extroverts like having people around, but introverts need time alone. Extroverts thrive by engaging with others, but introverts thrive by processing events internally. Square relationships are intrinsically difficult, as those involved have different temperaments.

The square aspect also links elements that are incompatible: fire and earth, fire and water, air and water, or air and earth. Depending on the exact combination of elements, some of these relationships will be more problematic than others. Air with water is probably the most challenging square because thinking (air) and feeling (water) evaluate their experiences differently. Water/feeling is right-brained and subjective while air/thinking is left-brained and objective. Similarly, fire/intuition is right-brained and spontaneous, while earth/sensation is left-brained, more measured and rational.

Because fire and water share a right-brain focus and air and earth have a left-brain approach, these squares are usually less challenging, but all squares create tension because they link signs with the same quality. A good way to describe these tense relationships is cardinal conflicts, fixed feuds and mutable misunderstandings.

Cardinal conflicts arise because it's natural for cardinal signs to want to take the lead. When you have two people in a relationship who both want to take charge and make the decisions, who ends up being the leader? Couples can have disputes regarding life's priorities and the direction they want their lives to take. Is career or family more important? How do we prioritise? Give and take can become an issue in these relationships. How do we reach an agreement on a plan of action? Is it always the same person who must compromise and give way? Eventually, these difficulties can lead to a breakdown in cardinal relationships.

Fixed feuds are arguably the most entrenched disputes of all. When you have two people who are both convinced they are right, who will not give an inch of ground and who will not negotiate, or even consider alternatives, a stalemate situation can develop. Fixed signs are determined. When you have a relationship between two people who are equally persistent and unwilling to change, there is no middle ground. When taken to extremes, anger, hostility and even violence can develop.

Mutable misunderstandings are not quite as fraught, but they are still challenging. Because mutable signs are by nature adaptable, there is often more willingness to compromise and discuss issues. But communication problems are common in mutable square relationships and often come down to a matter of perspective. Gemini and Virgo are detail-focused and have a left-brain emphasis, but Gemini is an extroverted sign while Virgo is introverted. Sagittarius and Pisces tend to see the big picture and have a right brain emphasis, but Sagittarius is the extrovert and Pisces is the introvert. Difficulties in mutable relationships can lead to instability and a lack of direction.

In storytelling, the square aspect corresponds to crossing the first adventure threshold where the hero must make a commitment to their journey. It's a point of decisive action and calls for courage. It requires a leap into the unknown. There is often an encounter with a threshold guardian who tests your protagonist. The issues heroes face at this first threshold, might recur. At the opposition, which aligns with the supreme ordeal, heroes will again face another trial and again when they reach the resurrection phase of their journey. When they return home to their 'ordinary world', how has their journey transformed them?

Trines

Harmonious signs: The same polarity, the same element, different quality.

Trines are happy, comfortable relationships between signs with a lot in common. These signs enjoy one another's company and like to spend time together. They understand each other. Even so, all relationships can have a degree of challenge. The differences in their qualities are the main areas where they will encounter some discomfort.

Cardinal signs can find fixed signs too slow to act and they can have issues with mutable signs, who they sometimes view as being too inconsistent. Fixed signs can find mutable signs too chaotic and changeable and think that cardinal signs are too bossy and controlling. Mutable signs sometimes think that cardinal signs are too domineering and can view fixed signs as inflexible, stubborn, or slow. But trine aspects are harmonious connections, so these issues are usually minor irritations.

Signs that are 120 degrees apart evoke the energy of fire. This is because Leo and Sagittarius are both 120 degrees away from 0 Aries, which is also a fire sign and the start of the zodiac. Fire is creative, expressive and dynamic, so all trine aspects evoke these qualities. Trine relationships are usually comfortable and stable, but they can sometimes become very one-track. For example, in fire-fire relationships, the two individuals can be ultra-competitive with one another. Fire signs are extroverted, active and independent. Fire is warm, generous and expressive, but too much fire can get out of control and become destructive, consuming vast amounts of fuel to keep burning.

In air-air trines, there can be a lot of time spent engaging in social interactions with friends and colleagues outside the relationship. Air is the most sociable element. Like fire, it is extroverted and naturally outgoing and expressive, but when there is too much air, a flighty, superficial situation can develop. Over time, air trine relationships can burnout because of the fiery nature of the trine itself, which can consume air. Once the initial excitement of a new social relationship passes, there's nothing to sustain it. Without ongoing fuel, there is no reason for the connection to exist.

Earth signs are practical and down-to-earth. These relationships are inherently stable and engender a feeling of security. In earth-earth combinations, partners can become overly focused on their work and making money and over time, these relationships can become rather dull and routine. The intrinsic fiery nature of the trine relationship can scorch the earth, leaving it dry and devoid of life.

Water signs are deep and emotional. When there is too much water, as can happen in water-water trines, partners can become overly sensitive, sentimental, or emotionally needy. The trine aspect, being naturally fiery in nature, can cause water to boil, leading to emotional instability.

But all trine problems are relatively minor. These relationships are generally long-lived and comfortable and provide opportunities to resolve these differences. Signs in trine provide a high degree of mutual understanding. Partners feel they are 'in their element'.

Quincunxes

Strange signs: Different polarity, different element, different quality.

Like the semi-sextile, these signs have neither polarity, nor element, nor quality in common, but unlike the semi-sextile, they are 150 degrees apart, so there is no cusp to connect them. If we want to get to know these people, we must go on a strange journey to an unfamiliar place.

In terms of the hero's journey, quincunxes are close to the supreme ordeal, near the opposition. We're in strange territory here. The landscape is unfamiliar. At this point in your story, your main character is likely to encounter a shapeshifter who creates confusion, uncertainty and danger. In the 1979 movie *Alien*, the crew of *Nostromo* investigates a derelict spaceship of unknown origin. Inside, they find a chamber filled with strange eggs. A creature hatches and leaps onto Kane's face. After returning to their ship, Kane seems to recover, but then suddenly a horrifying creature bursts from his chest, killing him. Soon the alien grows into a monstrous and aggressive creature called the Xenomorph and we know that the supreme ordeal for the rest of the crew is about to begin.

Quincunx aspects take us to a place where we feel extremely uncomfortable. We've never been here before and it's likely to be inhabited by folk who are totally alien to us. Their way of life, their values and personal preferences are incomprehensible. We don't understand these people and don't know what's happening.

There are two quincunxes that lie either side of the opposition. The opposition is a point where we can potentially reconcile these opposing energies, but it's also a point of crisis. It's through the opposition that we really learn about other people and we also learn about ourselves.

Oppositions

Confronting signs: The same polarity, compatible element, the same quality.

Oppositions are like encountering a magnetic mirror. These people draw us in, but they also reflect back to us. The opposition aspect delivers pivotal events and brings powerful people into our lives. We cannot ignore them. Often in relationships, we encounter the same recurring themes again and again.

Astrologically, these signs have a lot in common and seem to understand one another. Like sextiles, they have elements that are compatible, but because they share the same quality, be it cardinal, fixed or mutable, difficulties often arise. Opposition relationships have a particular energy that other aspects do not; they both attract and repel.

It's well-known that opposites attract. In a way, we are destined to encounter our opposing sign. They are like our shadow. Psychologically speaking, the shadow contains the unconscious parts of our psyche. We might think that the shadow is dark and evil, but the shadow contains both good and bad, positive and negative attributes. It's the same with oppositions.

Signs that oppose one another are in conflict because they have the same quality and yet we have some understanding and empathy for these signs. We want to stand by our opposite number in times of need, but we are still in conflict with them. Conflicts tend to arise simply because the relationship exists.

These contradictions make opposition relationships intrinsically difficult. Love-hate scenarios, issues around give and take, parent-child issues, decision-making problems and a range of confrontations can develop. Because we are magnetically connected to our opposing sign, we can't seem to let go, nor do we want to.

In storytelling, this is where we reach a major turning point. It's where heroes face their greatest test, the supreme ordeal. This ordeal is really a confrontation with one's own shadow self. Whatever the connection – friends, lovers, colleagues, or family members – to some extent, all relationships evoke the energy of the opposition aspect. It's through our interactions with other people that we grow and evolve, which is the whole point of our journey. We learn from experiences and, along the way, develop more awareness of others and of ourselves.

Aspects, Angles and Archetypes
– Stages in the Hero's Journey

Aspects are one of the key components that inform astrological interpretations. There are many ways to integrate astrological aspects with your characters, their relationships with one another and the events in your story. Amazingly, aspects correlate with the stages in the hero's journey and can describe the situations and characters your protagonist encounters along the way. If you are using the template of the hero's journey to construct your story, exploring these scenarios will help you develop your narrative. In this section we'll focus on the planet Mars, but keep in mind that while the archetypal hero is male and Mars is traditionally the mythic figure associated with the hero, of course, this doesn't mean all heroes are male.

The Conjunction – 0 degrees –The Hero

When two planets are together in a conjunction, your main protagonist is in their known world. This is the starting point for their journey. This is a place of comfort, support and security. Who is your hero? Where are they? Where do they come from? Consider which zodiac sign best describes them.

1. *The First Semi-Sextile 30 degrees – The Herald.*
The Herald is a person (or event) who announces the call to adventure. To begin their journey, heroes must step outside their ordinary world to a place that is unfamiliar. The semi-sextile aspect introduces the reader to the unknown because these signs of the zodiac have nothing in common. At first, this step might seem harmless enough, or it may be treacherous and involve a major

commitment. Perhaps it's not very far to go, but those who live here are strangers. This is just the first step and your hero or heroine may be hesitant to embark on this journey. Why are they undertaking this adventure?

2.   *The First Semi-Square – 45 degrees – The Separation.*
This aspect takes place when the hero (Mars) must say goodbye to his lover (Venus). Venus cannot travel with him; she must stay behind and wait for his return. While many traditional stories mirror this classic model, in your story it might be the female protagonist who is on the heroic journey and her male lover who stays behind, or it might be a same sex union, or a non-sexual connection. Whatever the scenario, this is a point of separation for your hero.

3.   *The First Sextile – 60 degrees – Sidekicks and Helpers.*
The sextile is a helpful aspect and fits neatly with this archetype and this stage in the hero's journey. Sidekicks offer assistance and support. The friends your hero encounters along the way can provide information about what to expect on the road ahead. Sextile aspects are about communication, so your hero might learn some important facts, find a map, or receive a special gift that will help them navigate the terrain they will encounter.

4.   *The First Square – 90 degrees – Threshold Guardians.*
Crossing the threshold is the first major challenge for your protagonist. This encounter sets the scene for the problems your hero will face. Characters and events at this threshold activate a square aspect and will evoke the same quality as your hero, whether cardinal, fixed or mutable. Here, heroes often meet Threshold Guardians, or gatekeepers who set hard tasks for the hero. These obstacles test your hero's commitment to the journey and their ability to face the coming ordeal.

5. *The First Trine – 120 degrees – Allies, Advisors, Mentors.*
Trine aspects connect signs with the same astrological element, so characters connected by trine have a similar viewpoint and approach to life. With the same element as your hero, whether it's fire, earth, air or water, these Allies understand what your hero is facing and offer guidance, friendship, support and helpful advice.

6. *The First Sesquisquare – 135 degrees – Standstill and Turning Point.*
When Mars is 135 degrees from the Sun, he appears to stop and then move backwards. This apparent station and ensuing retrograde motion symbolise an important stage in the hero's journey. Mars can feel powerless when stationary and he is about to face his greatest challenges while retrograde. These tests will strengthen your hero and lead to resilience and determination, but they can also bring defeat and loss. Heroes must dig deep within their psyche to find the mental, emotional and physical strength to undertake this journey. This is a key turning point in your story.

7. *The First Quincunx – 150 degrees – Shapeshifters.*
This aspect links zodiac signs that have nothing in common. They have different polarities, qualities and elements. This aspect thrusts your hero into the unknown, a place where strange characters reside. When heroes encounter people and experiences associated with the quincunx, they are out of their depth. They are alone and feel lost. Shapeshifters constantly change their form and point of view. They can take on the guise of a seducer who tempts your hero or lures them into a labyrinth of confusion. Shapeshifters are unpredictable and deceptive.

8. *The Opposition – 180 degrees – The Shadow.*
In Jungian psychology, the Shadow archetype represents unconscious aspects of the hero. This part of the journey aligns with the Supreme

Ordeal, where your hero will confront their principal antagonist. This antagonist often represents something the hero is avoiding and which they need to incorporate into their own psyche. A planet or sign opposing the conscious ego is often projected onto others, so unconscious traits and emotions are met head-on. Opposing signs have the same quality, be it cardinal, fixed or mutable, so they are challenging, but they also have compatible elements, which can assist the hero by suggesting ways to work through these challenges and integrate the unconscious shadow material.

9.   *The Second Quincunx – 150 degrees – The Trickster.*
Once again, the hero finds themselves in a strange place. They are a long way from home and trying to make sense of their experiences. Here, the hero can encounter tricksters who are clever, but also deceitful. There is often an element of fun amid the chaos they can create. Tricksters force your hero to adapt and change. Although the quincunx represents the unknown, this is the second time they have been in this situation, so by now, they should have learned something. Tricksters force your hero to learn.

10.   *The Second Sesquisquare – 135 degrees – Standstill.*
       Another Turning Point.
The 135-degree aspect is again in play. Mars is once again stationary and about to turn direct once more. Heroes have been through an ordeal and can feel vulnerable. Introspection is not a normal process for Mars, who is always looking for action and adventure, but to move ahead while feeling wounded is yet another test and this one requires some soul searching. Inner reflection can lead to a turning point that reveals the path forward. Between the Trickster and the Mentor, this is where the hero learns the truth about others and, importantly, more about himself. This standstill is an opportunity for integration.

11.   *The Second Trine – 120 degrees – Allies, Advisors, Mentors.*
Like the first trine, this aspect represents characters who offer support, guidance and good advice. As this is the second trine, these characters are often teachers or sages who can offer a higher level of support and wise counsel to your hero. They set an example for the hero to emulate. Your hero might meet the same advisor they met at the first trine and who acknowledges how far they have come. There are still further tests ahead, so heroes still need to listen to sage advice.

12.   *The Second Square – 90 degrees – Crossing the Threshold Again.*
Once more, the hero faces challenges associated with the square aspect. This time, having had experiences that have elevated their understanding, they can potentially overcome these issues. Are they ready to take this step? Cardinal conflicts, fixed feuds and mutable misunderstandings once again arise. The Threshold Guardian is a character who sets tasks for the hero to master before they can step across the threshold and begin the journey home.

13.   *The Second Sextile – 60 degrees – Sidekicks and Helpers.*
The transformation of your hero is complete and he is now journeying home. This aspect provides a message for your main protagonist. With all they have learned, how can they use this knowledge to help others? Your hero could also receive a reward for all their hard work, be it a material gift, or the gift of knowledge. They might encounter those who have previously helped them on their journey and can now reciprocate by assisting them and their communities.

14.   *The Second Semi-Square – 45 degrees – Return to Love.*
On the road home, the hero often reaches a point where he is reunited with his lover. But at this reunion, there comes a realisation

that they have both changed. The journey has transformed your hero. Meanwhile, his lover has not been sitting idle but has had their own experiences and tests as part of their journey. Can the relationship continue? The reunion may not go according to plan. To continue, the nature of the relationship must change, too. This is a point of transformation.

15.   *The Second Semi-Sextile – 30 degrees – The Herald Returns.*
Nearing home, your protagonist now embodies the Herald archetype, announcing their homecoming. Your hero has become a catalyst for change and can help their community and loved ones solve their problems. Everything your hero has experienced has fostered wisdom and self-knowledge. Are they humble? Do they feel superior? Is the community ready to listen? Your hero might feel like a stranger, no longer feeling they are part of their home, family or community.

16.   *The Conjunction – 0 degrees – The Homecoming.*
Returning home after a long adventure is a time for rest and recuperation. It's also about psychological integration. The journey has transformed your hero, so although they are home, they are not really in the same place or state of mind. They have evolved. The wisdom they have gained means they are different. They have developed knowledge of the world and of themselves, so now another journey is about to begin.

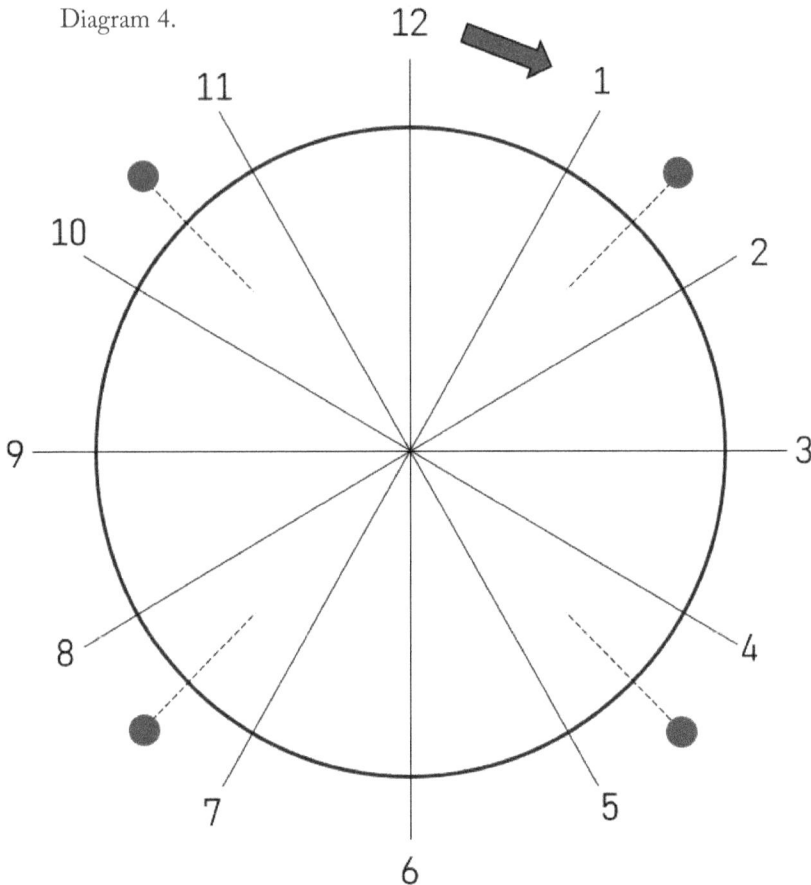

Diagram 4. - Mars starts his heroic journey when conjunct the Sun at the number 12 position. From there, he travels in the direction of the arrow. Follow the numbers to gain further insight into astrological aspects and how they mirror the stages of the hero's journey. Note that the 45-degree and 135-degree aspects are shown by dots, not numbers.

Relationship Aspects

Sign	Conjunction 0° Matching Allies Ordinary World	Semi-sextile 30° Unfamiliar Heralds Call to Adventure	Sextile 60° Helpful Sidekicks Guidance	Square 90° Conflicting Enemies Challenges/Tests	Trine 120° Harmonious Mentors Advisors	Quincunx 150° Strange Shapeshifters Tricksters	Opposition 180° Confronting Shadows Ordeals
Aries	Aries	Taurus/Pisces	Gemini/Aquarius	Cancer/Capricorn	Leo/Sagittarius	Virgo/Scorpio	Libra
Taurus	Taurus	Gemini/Aries	Cancer/Pisces	Leo/Aquarius	Virgo/Capricorn	Libra/Sagittarius	Scorpio
Gemini	Gemini	Cancer/Taurus	Leo/Aries	Virgo/Pisces	Libra/Aquarius	Scorpio/Capricorn	Sagittarius
Cancer	Cancer	Leo/Gemini	Virgo/Taurus	Libra/Aries	Scorpio/Pisces	Sagittarius/Aquarius	Capricorn
Leo	Leo	Virgo/Cancer	Libra/Gemini	Scorpio/Taurus	Sagittarius/Aries	Capricorn/Pisces	Aquarius
Virgo	Virgo	Libra/Leo	Scorpio/Cancer	Sagittarius/Gemini	Capricorn/Taurus	Aquarius/Aries	Pisces
Libra	Libra	Scorpio/Virgo	Sagittarius/Leo	Capricorn/Cancer	Aquarius/Gemini	Pisces/Taurus	Aries
Scorpio	Scorpio	Sagittarius/Libra	Capricorn/Virgo	Aquarius/Leo	Pisces/Cancer	Aries/Gemini	Taurus
Sagittarius	Sagittarius	Capricorn/Scorpio	Aquarius/Libra	Pisces/Virgo	Aries/Leo	Taurus/Cancer	Gemini
Capricorn	Capricorn	Aquarius/Sagittarius	Pisces/Scorpio	Aries/Libra	Taurus/Virgo	Gemini/Leo	Cancer
Aquarius	Aquarius	Pisces/Capricorn	Aries/Sagittarius	Taurus/Scorpio	Gemini/Libra	Cancer/Virgo	Leo
Pisces	Pisces	Aries/Aquarius	Taurus/Capricorn	Gemini/Sagittarius	Cancer/Scorpio	Leo/Libra	Virgo

This table shows the angular relationships (aspects) between each sign of the zodiac: the conjunction, semi-sextile, sextile, square, trine, quincunx and opposition.[10]

4. GENERATIONAL AND HISTORICAL INFLUENCES

Pluto and Neptune travel very slowly through the zodiac. Their orbits of 248 and 165 years respectively are much longer than a human lifespan. Because of this, these two planets symbolise collective events and processes. Everyone born into these generations carries the imprint of Pluto's and Neptune's sign positions. Those within each era grow up amid a set of global influences and events that shape their development.

Whether your story is set in the past, the present, or the future, the symbolism of the zodiac sign where these slow-moving planets are located is a backdrop where you can place your characters. Using the images associated with Pluto's and Neptune's sign will deliver an atmosphere that resonates with your audience and engages your readers, and it can help you understand the events that have shaped your protagonist's worldview.

Because Pluto and Neptune move so slowly, there is often an overlapping retrograde period when these planets are transitioning from one sign to another. These transitional periods can last a few years. They are often pivotal years when significant paradigm shifts take place.

Pluto

Everyone has heard of Baby Boomers, the generation born after World War II, when the population boomed. Then came Generation X, the Millennials and a host of other generations grouped together according to certain timelines and characteristics. These population categories were first devised by Neil Howe and William Strauss.

Astrology has its own arrangement for generational groups, which is based on the sign occupied by Pluto. Pluto symbolises death and rebirth. It operates as a process of social transformation that foreshadows endings and beginnings beyond our control. These events play out according to the symbolism of the sign where Pluto is located and influence those born within each Pluto generation. While there are countless events happening every day across the world, in this section, we will focus on examples from European and Western history, which are widely documented in our culture.

Pluto in Aries

1333–63

1579–1609

1822–53

Over the past 1000 years, whenever Pluto has been moving through Aries, it has made a conjunction with the maverick planet, Uranus. These conjunctions have fuelled the dynamic conditions that can erupt at these intervals. These alignments have added to the potential for violence we see when Pluto traverses the sign ruled by Mars, the god of war. When Pluto and Uranus unite and especially when they converge in Aries, they deliver a powerful revolutionary energy. Outer planet conjunctions like this foreshadow systemic political and social transformation.

Aries likes to assert itself and Pluto wants control, so the combination of these archetypes can generate a desire for conquest, domination and independence.

In 1848, political revolutions swept across many parts of Europe, including Ireland, Germany, Italy and Belgium. There was a push for independence in many regions including Greece, Mexico, Texas, Costa Rica, Ecuador and Peru.

In America and Australia, this was the era of gunslingers and bushrangers. Rugged pioneers explored fresh territory, overrunning indigenous populations and paving the way for developers who would soon build new towns and cities when Pluto moved into Taurus.

Those born with Pluto in Aries are often trailblazers and revolutionaries, and their stories often reflect these themes. Writers born with Pluto in Aries include Emily Dickinson, Lewis Carroll, Thomas Hardy, Robert Louis Stevenson and Jules Verne.

Historic Events

1337	The Hundred Years War begins, lasting 116 years.
1347–51	Black Death. The bubonic plague kills millions.
1588	The English defeat the Spanish Armada.
1600	The East India Company founded.
1605	The Gunpowder Plot, the attempted assassination of King James I.
1839–42	The first Opium War.
1846–48	Mexican–American War.
1848	Revolutions sweep Europe.

Pluto in Taurus

1363–97

1608–41

1851–84

Owing to its elliptical orbit, Pluto spends more time in Taurus than any other zodiac sign. Pluto in Taurus fosters investment in industry and emphasises economic development and material security.

There can be a siege mentality to this mix of archetypes. It will simply not give up or give in. Pluto in Taurus wants permanence and it has an intense survival instinct. Material security and the desire for money and wealth feature strongly in these years.

In 14th century Europe and England, in the aftermath of the plague, there were few peasants left to work the land. Consequently, the feudal system began to fall apart. Wealthy landowners no longer held all the power.

From 1608 to 1641, Pluto again spent many years slowly traversing Taurus terrain when the obstinate English ruler, Charles I, came to power in 1625. His reign fostered a long-standing dispute with the English parliament, which would lead to the English Civil War and Charles' eventual downfall and beheading in 1649.

During this period, the transatlantic slave trade intensified. Driven by greed and exploitation, slavery stoked economic growth for European colonial powers. Countless Africans were enslaved and shipped across the Atlantic. In 1861, one full cycle of Pluto later, the American Civil War broke out. The southern states did not want to abolish slavery, as it was the mainstay of their economy, but change was coming.

Just as Pluto was entering Taurus around 1850, gold was discovered in California and in Australia. In both regions, gold spurred economic development and boosted trade and investment. There was a massive expansion of railways to transport manufactured goods, distribute food and carry passengers. Across the world, developers acquired large tracts of land to facilitate the construction of infrastructure.

Writers born with Pluto in Taurus include George Bernard Shaw, James Joyce, Thomas Mann, John Milton and Oscar Wilde.

Historic Events

1378–1417	The Great Schism split the Catholic Church.
1381	The Peasants' Revolt. Serfs demand an end to the feudal system.
1607	First colonial settlement in North America at Jamestown, Virginia.
1620	Pilgrims aboard the Mayflower settle in Plymouth, Massachusetts.
1618–48	The Thirty Years War.
1850–51	Gold rush began in California and Australia.
1853–56	Crimean War.
1861–65	American Civil War.
1869	Suez Canal completed.

Pluto in Gemini

1396–1425

1640–70

1882–1914

To trace the significance of this cycle, we need to go back to the year 1399 when Pluto made a conjunction with Neptune. This conjunction in Gemini marked a new epoch. The 1399 conjunction of Neptune and Pluto was the first one in Gemini since pre-history and heralded a radical shift in our collective development. It brought about the decline of land-based feudal and agricultural systems (Taurus) and thrust civilisation into a new information era.

The most important singular advance at this time was Johannes Gutenberg's invention of the printing press[11], which fostered literacy, education and the spread of information, sparking the Renaissance.

Pluto was again in Gemini from 1640 to 1670 when newspapers became more commonplace.[12] The London Gazette was first published in 1665 and news sheets spread throughout Europe.

The most recent Neptune-Pluto conjunction in Gemini occurred in 1891–92, when tremendous advances in the Gemini fields of communication and transportation ushered in the 20th century. Tesla, Curie, Edison, Marconi, Einstein and Bell were some of the great minds whose inventions and discoveries opened the door to our modern era. Inventions like the electric light, radio, flight, X-rays and the motor car revolutionised the Gemini fields of communication and transportation. Nikola Tesla's pioneering work in alternating current paved the way for the electrification of homes and cities. These breakthroughs transformed society. In keeping with the symbolism of Gemini, a plethora of new gadgets and electrical devices, such as toasters, vacuum cleaners and washing machines, soon followed.

Writers born with Pluto in Gemini include Agatha Christie, Dorothy Parker, Ernest Hemingway, TS Eliot and Tennessee Williams.

Historic Events

1660	Royal Society founded.
1665–66	Great Plague of London.
1666	Great Fire of London.
1891	Major advances herald a new era of communication and transport.

Pluto in Cancer

1425–48

1669–94

1912–39

Cardinal water sign Cancer is the sign of home and family. It's no surprise that these themes feature prominently when Pluto's transformative power makes its presence felt so close to home. Pluto was in Cancer from 1425 to 1448 when the powerful Medici family came to prominence in Florence, Italy. Beginning in 1434 with the rise to power of Cosimo de Medici, the family made Florence the centre of the Renaissance.

In 1689, during the next era of Pluto in Cancer, a new dynasty came to the English throne. The Glorious Revolution of 1688 was a bloodless event that resulted in the overthrow of King James II and the establishment of William III and Mary II as monarchs.

Pluto moved into Cancer just as the First World War flared in Europe. The spark that ignited hostilities, the 1914 assassination of Archduke Francis Ferdinand, took place when Pluto had just crossed into Cancer. Young men eagerly signed up for military service. The underlying feeling was that one was fighting for one's country, one's homeland (Cancer). Millions of people were killed. Millions more were wounded and suffered permanent disabilities. Separated from their homes and loved ones, families were torn apart. The Russians suffered more than most, enduring cold, starvation and disease as fuel and food shortages sparked the Bolshevik uprising. For many, worse was to come. If these horrors weren't enough, the worldwide Spanish flu pandemic killed millions more. Uprooted from their homes and having lost many family members, those who survived felt a deep sense of loss, spawning a desperate need for security. People born in this generation became very security-conscious. They carried within them the imprint of the displacement and material hardship that took place in these tough years.

Pluto was discovered in 1930 and named for the lord of the underworld, which added significantly to the trials of this time. When planets are discovered and named, the associated themes and symbols of that archetype become more apparent. One wonders how different history might have been if Pluto had been given a different name, something more uplifting and hopeful.

A long period of economic hardship and disruption followed Pluto's discovery. With the 1929 stock market crash, the world was thrust into the Great Depression. Basic necessities like food and shelter were in short supply. There was widespread homelessness.

Writers born with Pluto in Cancer include Alex Haley, Jack Kerouac, Truman Capote and Colleen McCullough.

Historic Events

1428–29	Joan of Arc leads the French to victory in the siege of Orleans.
1688	The Glorious Revolution.
1914–18	World War I.
1917	The Russian Revolution.
1918–19	Spanish Flu pandemic.
1930s	The Great Depression.

Pluto in Leo

1447–65

1693–1711

1937–58

Leo is a regal sign where Pluto's presence delivers revolutionary events that play out across empires and within the seats of power. Leo's ruling planet is the Sun, the centre of the solar system and the head of creative energy and power, but as Pluto is in the darkest reaches of space, this intense contrast of light and dark symbolises the opposing forces which can manifest when Pluto is in Leo.

Pluto was in Leo from 1447 to 1465, where it united with Uranus in 1455–56. The Turks captured Constantinople in 1453, founding the Ottoman Empire. In the same year, the Hundred Years War between France and England finally came to an end and The War of the Roses began.

Pluto was in Leo again from 1693 to 1711 when Uranus and Pluto met in conjunction in 1710. The War of Spanish Succession 1701–1714 was not just a European conflict but spread across the Atlantic as colonial powers fought for control over North, Central and South America. This era covered the latter part of the long rule of Louis XIV of France (1643–1715). At 72 years, this is still the longest reign of any sovereign in history, consistent with the fixed nature of Leo and of Scorpio, the sign ruled by Pluto.

Pluto entered Leo at the beginning of World War II. With leadership a key theme of this regal sign, this period saw the rise of powerful dictators, Hitler, Mussolini and Stalin. Meanwhile, in the US, Franklin D. Roosevelt served as President from 1933 until his death in 1945. He's the only US President to have served more than two successive terms. In keeping with the fixed sign Leo, many people born in this generation have held leadership roles throughout the 20th century and beyond.

In 1938, nuclear fission led to the development of nuclear weapons. Humanity witnessed the blinding terror of the dawning of the nuclear age and the Cold War. Pluto's modern rulership of fixed sign Scorpio galvanised in fixed sign Leo, resulting in an entrenched and long-lasting stand-off.

The Pluto in Leo generation (1937–58) closely aligns with the Baby Boomer generation (1946–64), who have cemented their social influence and control. The sign of Leo is associated with creativity, including procreation, so it's not surprising there was a population explosion in this era.

Writers born with Pluto in Leo include Michael Crichton, Germaine Greer, Samuel Johnson, Erica Jong and Stephen King.

Historic Events

1453	Fall of the Byzantine Empire. Ottomans capture of Constantinople.
1453	End of the Hundred Years War.
1701–14	War of Spanish Succession.
1939–45	World War II.
1945	Atomic bombs destroy Hiroshima and Nagasaki.
1950s	Cold War.

Pluto in Virgo

1465–78

1711–25

1956–72

Unlike the broad Leo realms of empires and kingdoms, Virgo is more focused on details. Virgo is an industrious and hardworking sign. It's interested in efficiency and communication, as well as health and hygiene. Pluto in Virgo transforms the world in a more personal way.

During the Renaissance, the focus was on symmetry and perfection. Leonardo da Vinci was born in 1452 and Michelangelo was born in 1475. Both men harnessed the energy of Pluto in Virgo to develop their skills and applied them across a wide range of arts and sciences. With the development of the printing press, literacy and information spread across Europe.

Pluto was next in Virgo from 1711 to 1725. In 1712, Thomas Newcomen developed his steam engine, which spawned the Industrial Revolution. At this time, there was growing awareness of the importance of sanitation and its vital role in preventing disease. In 1721, the first pharmacopoeia was published in London, marking a step toward standardising medical practices.

During the 1956–72 period, rates of unemployment were low in most developed countries and women began to make up a much larger percentage of the workforce. Productivity was high. Computers began to revolutionise the workplace and there were also important advances in the Virgo realms of health and healing, including the first organ transplants and the first artificial heart.

The Uranus-Pluto conjunction of 1966 was pivotal, seeding a tremendous social revolution. It was the time of the Vietnam War and the growing peace movement, which would eventually bring an end to the conflict when Pluto shifted into peaceful Libra. The 60s were powerful times of sudden and shocking events. Martin Luther King, JFK and Robert Kennedy were assassinated. In China, Mao Zedong launched the Cultural Revolution. In 1969, Britain sent troops to Northern Ireland. Ongoing violence escalated, leading to Bloody Sunday in January 1972. In 1968, riots and protests erupted in Chicago and Paris. These were turbulent times across the globe.

When Uranus and Pluto are together, they manifest with tremendous energy and force. On 2 July 1966, France began its 30-year-long nuclear testing program at Mururoa Atoll. Uranus and Pluto were incredibly close to one another when the first bomb was detonated.

The generation born with Pluto in Virgo (1956–1972) has experienced widespread social change. Women of this era were the first generation to opt for a professional career over marriage and motherhood. With the advent of the contraceptive pill, which became available in the 1960s, women were free to devote themselves to their careers. The Women's Liberation Movement challenged traditional gender roles. Women of this generation are self-sufficient and value their independence. This group and the Pluto in Libra cohort share many traits with Generation X (1965–80).

Notable writers born with Pluto in Virgo include Nicolaus Copernicus, Carrie Fisher, Stephen Fry, Immanuel Kant, Thomas More and Adam Smith.

Historic Events

1710	The first British copyright act.
1711–12	Publication of *The Spectator*.
1957	European Economic Community founded.
1961	Berlin Wall constructed.
1962	The Cuban Missile Crisis.
1969	Apollo 11, the first manned mission to land on the Moon.

Pluto in Libra

1478–91

1724–37

1971–84

Libra's focus is on fairness, equality and justice. In times past, religious leaders enacted many of the first laws and the church was the centre of political power. Initially, laws were based on the teachings set down in the Bible. The Ten Commandments and other moral codes formed a framework the church used to impose its authority. In 1233, a year when Pluto entered Libra, the Catholic Church established the first Inquisition. The notorious Spanish Inquisition commenced in 1478, again when Pluto entered Libra.

Between 1724 and 1737, power began to shift away from monarchies and the church towards democratic systems where people elected their leaders and parliament made the laws.

Most recently, Pluto was in Libra from 1971 to 1984. In the US, corruption was exposed with the Watergate scandal, leading to Nixon's impeachment and resignation. The Vietnam War came to an end in this period. This was the era of peace protests when equality, civil rights, gay rights and the women's movement gained momentum. It was a period of immense social transformation across the globe, a continuation of the counter-culture revolution sparked by the 1966 conjunction of Uranus in Pluto in Virgo. In the wake of the 1960s violence, as the '70s began, there was a strong desire for peace and harmony. Socially, personal relationships underwent massive changes; indeed, a sexual revolution was underway. 'Make Love Not War' was the mantra of this generation. With Pluto in peace-loving Libra, John Lennon (Sun in Libra) composed *Imagine, Give Peace a Chance* and *Power to the People* in this era.

In Australia, Gough Whitlam came to power in 1972 with a strong reform agenda. His government would establish Medicare, move to establish Aboriginal rights, legislate free education and introduce a host of laws which were immensely popular. Globally, equal rights for women were being introduced into law, but inequality still exists today. It was not until 1971, a year when Pluto shifted into Libra, that women in Switzerland could legally vote.

The Pluto in Libra generation shares similar values to Generation X (c. 1964–1980). In keeping with the symbolism of Libra, this cohort seeks harmony and equality in their dealings with others and a work-life balance.

Writers born with Pluto in Libra include Martin Luther, born in 1483, whose theses of complaint spawned the religious Reformation, and John Adams, an activist and diplomat, who became the second US President and who was a co-signatory to the Declaration of Independence.

Historic Events

1478	The Spanish Inquisition established.
1485	Fall of Richard III. Tudor dynasty established.
1725	Peter I dies and his wife Catherine I becomes Empress of Russia.
1972–74	Watergate scandal.
1975	End of the Vietnam War.

Pluto in Scorpio

1490–1502

1736–49

1983–95

'Greed is good,' says Gordon Gekko (Michael Douglas) in the 1987 movie *Wall Street*. The collective obsession in this era was money and power. Similarly, greed and corruption were evident between 1490 and 1502 when the Borgia dynasty was in power in Europe. Rodrigo Borgia (1431–1503) became Pope Alexander VI in 1492. He fathered many illegitimate children, including Lucrezia Borgia, who he manipulated for his own greedy interests. This era was a particularly dark time in the seat of Christian power. It was common knowledge that murder, incest, adultery and corruption were rife within the Papal States. These activities planted the seeds for the Reformation, which followed.

Between 1736 and 1749, when Pluto was next transiting Scorpio, colonialism reached its zenith. Motivated by greed and profit, the slave trade grew. It's estimated that over 10 million Africans were enslaved and transported across the Atlantic to the Americas, the majority in the 18th century.

In Scorpio, Pluto highlights fundamental issues of survival. Death is part of the symbolism of Pluto and of Scorpio and so is sex. In 1983, as Pluto slipped into its underworld home, HIV and AIDS first emerged. This transit of Pluto in its own sign started out with escalating corporate profiteering and high interest rates, which triggered a deep recession in the wake of the Black Monday Stock Market crash of October 1987. Boom and bust. This was an intense cycle, foreshadowing reversals of fortune.

Rebirth follows destruction. The end of communism in Europe and the end of apartheid in South Africa occurred in this era. These political changes were also seeded by Saturn, Neptune and Uranus, which were moving through Capricorn in the early 1990s.

This generational group closely mirrors the Millennials (c. 1981–96), many of whom have passionate political views. This cohort seeks to be in control of their own destiny and will stand up to those in authority. They are resilient. They can transform themselves to adapt to the ever-changing work scene, which helps them manage the job insecurity that followed economic privatisation. Those who have Pluto in Scorpio often undergo powerful transformative experiences. In their journey, these individuals must sometimes overhaul their lives completely and start over.

Notable writers born with Pluto in Scorpio include Thomas Jefferson and Johann Wolfgang von Goethe.

Historic Events

1492	Columbus reaches the Americas.
1492–1502	Age of Exploration.
1986	Chernobyl accident.
1989	Fall of the Berlin Wall.
1990–94	The end of apartheid in South Africa.
1989–93	The collapse of communism in Europe.
1989	Stock market crash.
1990–94	Recession.

Pluto in Sagittarius

1502–16

1748–63

1995–2008

The 1502–16 transit of Pluto in Sagittarius inspired widespread exploration. Ships travelled far and wide in search of gold and new trading partners. Europeans began colonial expansion. This brought about a massive clash of cultures, destruction and death within indigenous populations, both by intent and by the spread of diseases which were previously unknown in those regions. European explorers began a systematic invasion of North, Central and South America to 'civilise' the natives, destroying their traditional beliefs and forcing so-called 'Christian values' upon native populations. For the most part, the attitude of the Europeans was that this was for the natives' own good, to save them from hell and damnation. But clearly, people would not have set off on long, expensive and dangerous expeditions if there was nothing in it for them.

Consistent with the expansive nature of Sagittarius, during the transit of 1748–63, Europeans were arriving in vast numbers in the American colonies. King George III issued a proclamation prohibiting America from trading with any country except Britain, sowing the seeds of the American War of Independence.

The revolution in the Gemini fields of communications and transport in the late 19th century laid the foundation of our global culture. By the 1990s, with Pluto in the opposite sign, Sagittarius, further advances in communication technology emerged, including email, the Internet, mobile phones and the development of drones.

Pluto in Sagittarius tries to exert control and power over an ever-changing (mutable) landscape. Ruled by expansive Jupiter, Sagittarius can overstep its bounds as it strives to expand its scope and influence. Following the horrific 9/11 terrorist attacks in 2001, tighter laws governing immigration and customs were enacted. In 2003, the US-led coalition invaded and bombed Iraq, citing concerns about weapons of mass destruction, which ultimately proved to be unfounded. Refugees arriving on Australian shores were locked in immigration detention centres. People suspected of terrorism were imprisoned at Guantanamo Bay and held there for years without being charged and without access to legal representation.

Terrorism and the battle against it became the dominant global theme in this astrological era. In keeping with the symbolism of Sagittarius, this conflict was not between countries, but between competing ideologies, beliefs and cultural concepts without clear borders.

Pluto in Sagittarius saw religious groups make their presence felt in the political arena by throwing their support behind candidates. Meanwhile, media attention exposed the widespread sexual (Pluto) abuse by Catholic priests (Sagittarius).

The Pluto in Sagittarius generation, born 1995–2008, closely matches Generation Z (c. 1997–2010), who grew up with social media and, like Sagittarius, value education and honesty. Well-known writers born with Pluto in Sagittarius include William Blake, George Buchanan, Robert Burns and Mary Wollstonecraft.

Historic Events

1513   Vasco Núñez de Balboa the first European to reach the Pacific Ocean.

1748–63	Widespread colonial expansion across Asia, Africa and the Americas.
1995–2008	Global expansion of the Internet, email and mobile phone technology.
2000–2008	Social media revolution.
2001	The 9/11 terrorist attacks.

Pluto in Capricorn

1516–33

1762–78

2008–2024

Capricorn represents the systems upon which the fabric of civilisation rests. With Pluto in Capricorn, these fundamental structures can undergo powerful changes, which can undermine the civilised world.

An examination of tree rings and ice core samples from all over the world shows that planet Earth was subjected to an extremely cold period which began circa 536 CE and which lasted perhaps twenty years or more. This period has been called the Dark Ages because of the collapse of culture, but it seems it was literally dark because the sun had stopped shining. Crops failed; famine and plague spread. Superstition flourished. Empires fell. Scientists have uncovered evidence that this climatic catastrophe was most likely triggered by a massive volcanic eruption which caused a mini-ice age. Pluto entered Capricorn in the year 532 CE, just prior to this event, symbolising the destructive volcanic forces released from the underworld.

During the 1516–33 transit, the Spanish commander Pizarro captured the Inca Empire (1532). A few years earlier, Spanish invaders under the leadership of Cortez destroyed the Aztec Empire in 1517–21.

The Catholic Church was the most powerful institution in the 16th century. Throughout the entire transit of Pluto in Capricorn from 1516 to 1533, history was to witness a massive power shift and the utter collapse of the authority of Rome. Martin Luther first set the Reformation in motion when, just as Pluto began its transit of Capricorn in 1517, he challenged church authority by nailing his list of 95 complaints to the church door in Wittenberg, Germany. There was widespread outrage at the corruption within the Papal States.

Pluto was again in Capricorn from 1762 to 1778 when the last major colonial outpost was established in Australia and so began the destruction of yet another indigenous population and its culture by invading Europeans. The American Revolution took place at this time, followed by the Declaration of Independence, whilst James Watt's improved steam engine (1769) escalated the pace of the Industrial Revolution.

Pluto's most recent transit through Capricorn witnessed the fall of banks and institutions, which had appeared strong and unshakable. When the Global Financial Crisis spread across the world, it exposed widespread corruption and dysfunction within the corporate and financial sectors.

This transit of Pluto in Capricorn delivered a big reality check. We cannot keep using the Earth's resources at our current pace. Things must change to secure our long-term survival. Pluto in Capricorn asked us to cut back and be more ethical and conservative so we can preserve the Earth's resources in the wake of the climate emergency. While pressing us to live more sustainably, Pluto in Capricorn also undermined our trust in political systems and our leaders.

Another theme consistent with this transit is the ageing population, which is likely to put significant pressure on future financial budgets. Low birth rates in the West, combined with longevity, are causing a demographic shift of enormous proportions.

Those born with Pluto in Capricorn intrinsically understand the importance of the environment, aligning with the values of Generation Alpha (c. 2010–25). Writers born with Pluto in Capricorn include Jane Austen, Samuel Taylor Coleridge, Sir Walter Scott and William Wordsworth.

Historic Events

1517–33	The Reformation.
1522	The Magellan expedition completes first circumnavigation of the globe.
2008	Global Financial Crisis.
2011	Fukushima earthquake and tsunami.
2020–22	Covid pandemic.

Pluto in Aquarius

1532–54

1777–98

2023–44

Aquarius is a progressive sign interested in the future of humanity. Pluto here upturns the social order, sometimes suddenly and often irrevocably.

In 1543, Polish astronomer Nicolaus Copernicus set out his ideas concerning the heliocentric nature of the solar system in his work, *De Revolutionibus Orbium Coelestium*. It revolutionised the accepted thinking of the day.

With the Reformation spreading across Europe, Pluto in Aquarius dramatically affected religious worship. In England in 1532, Henry VIII defied Rome. His marriage to his first wife, Catherine of Aragon, was annulled and he married Anne Boleyn, establishing himself as the head of the Church of England. In January 1547, when Henry died, he was succeeded by his only son, nine-year-old Edward VI, who accelerated the agenda of religious reform. In 1549, the first English prayer book was introduced; at the time, this was a radical change.

With Pluto in Aquarius, the people of France rebelled and on 14 July 1789, stormed the Bastille, starting the French Revolution. 'Liberty, Equality, Fraternity' was the Aquarian rally cry of the day. Counter revolution and the Reign of Terror soon followed.

William Herschel discovered Uranus in 1781. This discovery shaped the desire for independence, new scientific concepts and the rebellious characteristics of this era. The Industrial Revolution was in full swing, forever altering the way of life for millions across the globe. The American Revolution, which commenced a few years earlier, was to continue throughout this turbulent cycle.

When Pluto began shifting into progressive Aquarius in early 2023, the future arrived at our door faster than we could have imagined. Breakthroughs in science and technology, such as artificial intelligence, quickly began altering many aspects of life. We are also experiencing changes in how we generate electricity and distribute power.

Pluto's presence in Aquarius is likely to overhaul many systems in dire need of modernisation. The world is undergoing another kind of industrial revolution as green technology and advances in robotics and computer technology transform our way of life.

Writers born with Pluto in Aquarius include Lord Byron, Mary Shelley, Percy Bysshe Shelley and John Keats.

Historic Events

1534	Henry VIII split with Rome and established the Church of England.
1542	Francis Xavier introduces Christianity to India.
1789	Storming of the Bastille.
1789–99	French revolution.
2023	Artificial intelligence emerges.
2023–44	Clean energy revolution.

Pluto in Pisces

1553–80

1797–1824

2043–69

Pluto in Pisces is a dark and mysterious combination of archetypes. Events that unfolded during the 1553–80 sojourn of Pluto in Pisces included significant upheavals concerning religion when many people were persecuted and put to death because of their faith.

In 1553, a few months after Pluto entered Pisces, the young King of England, Edward VI, died. There were fears of a return to Catholicism under Mary, Edward's half-sister, who was next in line to the throne. This led the dying King Edward and his lords to proclaim the unfortunate Lady Jane Grey as Queen. After nine days, Queen Jane and those who had supported her succession were deposed and executed. Mary's army took control and she was duly installed as Queen.

Initially popular with the people, sentiment soon changed. During her reign, Mary quickly re-established Catholicism in England and put to death over 300 'heretics'. Many were burned at the stake. Fortunately for those who avoided persecution, Bloody Mary didn't rule England for long. She died in 1558 at the age of 42. Her half-sister, Protestant Elizabeth I, was then crowned. Such was the hatred of Queen Mary I, England would never again be a Catholic nation.

During this era, there was widespread and ongoing conflict between Catholics and Protestants. In France, in 1572, the slaughter of around 25,000 French Protestants became known as the St Bartholomew Massacre. History paints Catherine de Medici as the agent of this slaughter. Meanwhile, in Russia, this period witnessed the reign of Ivan IV, the Terrible, whose brutal rule lasted from 1547 until 1584.

Creativity is a positive way to express Pluto in Pisces. William Shakespeare gained wide acclaim in his own lifetime. Many of his works contain dark themes which are highly charged with passionate imagery – betrayal, ruthlessness, devotion, power, murder, witchcraft, possession, madness, ghosts and spirits and a host of mythic themes which creatively convey Pluto in Pisces themes. His works have remained popular throughout the ages owing to these powerful archetypes.

In this era, Nostradamus published his cryptic predictions of apocalyptic destruction. His writings continue to intrigue us to this day, containing convoluted Piscean messages which are difficult to decipher.

Pluto was next in Pisces when on 5 April 1815, Mount Tambora in Indonesia erupted in a massive explosion which expelled around 150 cubic kilometres of ash, rising some 44 kilometres into the atmosphere. This volcanic material travelled around the globe and blocked the sun's rays. So powerful was this eruption that the following year, 1816, has been called the year without a summer. It snowed in Europe and the United States in summer that year. It was at this time when a young Mary Shelley wrote her epic tale, *Frankenstein*. In this dark fantasy, Shelley taps into the images and archetypes of Pluto in Pisces.

With Pluto traversing the last sign of the zodiac, we can find ourselves powerless in the face of immense archetypal events, which thrust large sections of humanity into transformative experiences. When we meet death and suffering on a mass scale, we can struggle to comprehend what has happened. We might blame God, or the planets, or karma, or fate, or the past collective actions of humanity. Following destructive cataclysms, people can undergo a profound spiritual transformation. Those who survive frequently experience a spiritual awakening (Neptune) amid the depths of grief (Pluto).

Writers born with Pluto in Pisces include Emily Brontë, Charles Dickens, Victor Hugo, Edgar Allan Poe, William Shakespeare and Alfred Lord Tennyson, and others who have explored these dark and gothic themes.

Historic Events

1553–58	Reign of Bloody Mary in England.
1558	Elizabethan era begins.
1804	Napoleon crowns himself Emperor.
1815	Battle of Waterloo.
1815	Mt Tambora in Indonesia erupts, affecting the global climate.

Neptune

Apart from the generational and revolutionary influences of Pluto, the sign where Neptune is located also evokes collective experiences and describes the ambience of each era. Neptune's sign inspires the music, fashion, art, trends and atmosphere of each period and illustrates the collective mood of the times. The position of Neptune also describes the themes and concepts expressed in the memorable books, music and movies which capture the collective imagination. I have listed some of the notable books published and the films released in each Neptunian period. These images and stories reflect the symbols and themes associated with Neptune's sign location.

Bear in mind that writers and filmmakers will be hard at work developing their material well before the release date. I have listed the publication dates and release dates, but writers often spend years developing their stories and screenplays. For example, the classic movie *The Godfather* was released in 1972 when Neptune had just shifted into Sagittarius, but it was written and produced when Neptune was in the underworld sign of Scorpio. Scorpio clearly describes the dark atmosphere, the sepia tones and, of course, the storyline.

Neptune in Aries

1534–49

1698–1713

1862–76

2025–39

The first cardinal point, the start of Aries, holds the promise of a fresh beginning. Mars rules Aries, so it's associated with direct action and initiative. However, Neptune does not possess these qualities. It has an affinity with watery Pisces, the last sign of the zodiac. This suggests that when Neptune is in Aries, we find ourselves at a critical intersection where endings and beginnings are happening simultaneously.

When Neptune crosses into the dynamic sign of Aries, it infuses collective dreams, ideals and beliefs with a passionate zeal. It also fosters the development of pioneers and trend-setters in artistic fields. As new concepts spread they challenge the status quo, as happened during the Protestant Reformation when Neptune was in Aries (1534–49). Under these conditions, people will rise and stand behind their leaders. The masses will fight for a cause they believe in.

This placement of Neptune can trigger ideological battles. In 1543, Copernicus published his theory outlining the heliocentric nature of the solar system, sparking widespread debate. Copernicus challenged (Aries) the long-standing beliefs (Neptune) that the Earth was the centre of creation. It is said that Copernicus finalised his manuscript on the day he died.

The publication *The Spectator* was first published in 1711 and 'sought to enliven morality with wit and temper wit with morality'.[13]

It was widely read and influenced public attitudes in both England and abroad. Many books published when Neptune is in Aries reflect its themes and topics, including *Alice's Adventures* (Aries) *in Wonderland* (Neptune) and Tolstoy's *War* (Aries) *and Peace* (Neptune).

People born during these years carry within them the imprint of these themes and symbols. HG Wells, author of *The War* (Aries) *of the Worlds* (Neptune), was born in 1866. Other writers born with Neptune in Aries include Winston Churchill, Benjamin Franklin, Samuel Johnson, Erik Satie and William Butler Yeats.

Notable Publications

Year	Title	Author
1536	*Institutes of the Christian Religion*	John Calvin
1543	*On the Revolutions of Heavenly Spheres*	Nicolaus Copernicus
1861	*Great Expectations*	Charles Dickens
1862	*Les Misérables*	Victor Hugo
1865	*Alice's Adventures in Wonderland*	Lewis Carroll
1867	*War and Peace*	Leo Tolstoy

Neptune in Taurus

1548–62

1712–26

1875–90

Neptune, the planet of imagination and dreams, becomes more practical and grounded when in the earthy sign of Taurus. Taurus is a creative placement for Neptune, which gives it form and substance. It provides avenues for the imagination to deliver tangible and lasting results.

During the 1712–26 sojourn of Neptune in Taurus, Johann Sebastian Bach composed his Brandenburg concertos (1711–20) and George Frideric Handel composed his Water Music collection. It's an especially beneficial cycle for music and the arts. The Impressionist movement flourished in the 1875–90 period, with works by Monet, Degas, Renoir, Van Gogh, Cezanne, Gauguin and others.

Neptune in Taurus inflates the desire for beauty, harmony and luxury. It can also promote a desire to gamble, but not for its thrills and adventure. This gambler is focused on financial reward and is more likely to speculate with a businesslike attitude and perhaps inside information. Still, that is no guarantee of success. Speculation can reach fever pitch, as it did in 1719–20 in England with the South Sea Bubble. When investors realised there was no substance to the company's wild claims (Neptune) of immense profits (Taurus), the stock price plummeted. This resulted in massive losses for investors who had bought shares at inflated prices. Many individuals lost their life savings.

Fashion in the 1712–26 period favoured the elaborate Baroque style. Highly decorative, sumptuous materials like silk and velvet were embellished with colourful embroidery, gold threads and beading. Baroque architecture from the period featured dramatic facades, intricate carvings and richly decorated interiors. If your story is set in this era, including descriptions of elaborate scenes and images will convey a feeling of opulence.

People born during these years carry within them the imprint of these themes and symbols. One of the key figures in the history of early cinema was Eadweard Muybridge. In the late 19th century, Muybridge conducted a series of experiments using multiple still cameras to create moving pictures of humans and animals. His work was the foundation for the motion picture industry. Writers born with Neptune in Taurus include Aleister Crowley, James Joyce, Carl Jung, Dorothea Mackellar, Thomas Mann and Adam Smith.

Notable Publications

1719	*Robinson Crusoe*	Daniel Defoe
1877	*Anna Karenina*	Leo Tolstoy
1879	*A Doll's House*	Henrik Ibsen
1883	*Treasure Island*	Robert Louis Stevenson
1885	*The Adventures of Huckleberry Finn*	Mark Twain
1890	*The Sign of Four*	Arthur Conan Doyle
1890	*The Picture of Dorian Gray*	Oscar Wilde

Neptune in Gemini

1561–75

1725–39

1889–1902

Neptune and Pluto meet at regular 492-year intervals (see Pluto in Gemini). The host of inventions and major advances that emerged in the Gemini realms of communication and travel during the most recent cycle (1889–1902) shaped the modern world. As the Victorian era came to an end, fashion trends reflected these shifts in lifestyle. For example, women were now riding bicycles (Gemini), which required more streamlined, simpler clothing.

The invention of wireless telegraphy and radio opened up new channels of communication. Synonymous with Neptune in Gemini, marketing and advertising first emerged in this era. Mass (Neptune) media (Gemini) provides us with information about world events, but also invites the potential for bias, which can easily skew the messages we are receiving.

Neptune in Gemini nourished the growth of the motion picture industry. Auguste and Louis Lumière are credited with the invention of the motion (Gemini) picture camera (Neptune) and the first public screening of films.

Ultimately, Neptune in Gemini challenges us to look beyond surface images to explore and investigate the unknown. Sir Arthur Conan Doyle created Sherlock Holmes in 1887, just as this cycle was about to commence. Besides his novels and over 50 short stories featuring Sherlock Holmes, Doyle wrote more than 1,000 essays and articles, exploring a range of Neptunian topics such as spiritualism and social issues. Interestingly, Doyle was born on May

22, when the Sun had just entered Gemini. By 1887, transiting Neptune was in the same position as his natal Sun, inspiring Doyle to create his detective, Sherlock Holmes.

People born during these years carry within them the imprint of these themes and symbols. William Shakespeare was born with Neptune in Gemini. Other notable writers born with Neptune in Gemini include: Agatha Christie, TS Eliot, F. Scott Fitzgerald, Henry Miller and Dorothy Parker.

Notable Publications

1726	*Gulliver's Travels*	Jonathan Swift
1739	*A Treatise of Human Nature*	David Hume
1892	*The Adventures of Sherlock Holmes*	Arthur Conan Doyle
1898	*The War of the Worlds*	HG Wells
1899	*The Interpretation of Dreams*	Sigmund Freud

Neptune in Cancer

1574–88

1738–52

1902–16

In the sign of Cancer, watery Neptune provides a supportive and sustaining environment. Personal security and family considerations are of paramount importance during this cycle. People want to feel secure.

Family, nationality, home: Neptune idealises these Cancerian themes. If we cannot find a measure of security in our present location or circumstances, Neptune in Cancer suggests where we might find it. The concept of the 'American Dream', signifying a land of prosperity and opportunity for all, became a common mantra during the 1902–1916 period. This wave of immigration saw 17.7 million people arrive in the United States.

Neptune and Cancer are both watery symbols. In the early part of the 20th century, shipbuilding was happening at breakneck speed. Companies competed with one another to create the biggest and best passenger liners. The promise of a magical experience on board these majestic vessels engaged the public imagination. The romance of the high seas motivated people of all classes to experience the wonders of ocean travel. Sadly, the Titanic disaster in 1912 took place in this era. When there is too much water, it seems we can float, swim or sink.

When we elevate the concept of home and family to the collective level, homeland and patriotic duty become romanticised. Such was the case at the start of World War I when so many young men rushed off to enlist.

Fantasy and romance are genres associated with Neptune in Cancer. If your story is set during these years, including watery imagery will help to create the right atmosphere.

People born with Neptune in Cancer carry within them the imprint of these themes and symbols. Writers who have Neptune in Cancer include: Daphne du Maurier, Simone de Beauvoir, Graham Greene, Johann Wolfgang von Goethe, Patrick White and Tennessee Williams.

Notable Publications

1747	*The Art of Cookery Made Plain and Easy*	Hannah Glasse
1749	*Tom Jones*	Henry Fielding
1902	*The Tale of Peter Rabbit*	Beatrix Potter
1903	*The Call of the Wild*	Jack London
1908	*The Wind in the Willows*	Kenneth Graeme
1913	*Sons and Lovers*	DH Lawrence
1913	*Pygmalion*	George Bernard Shaw
1915	*Of Human Bondage*	W. Somerset Maugham

Notable Films

1902	*A Trip to the Moon*

Neptune in Leo

1587–1602

1751–65

1915–29

Neptune in Leo links the elements water and fire, inflating the desire for love, pleasure and art. Neptune here is creative, self-interested and indulgent. When Neptune is in Leo, people want to have fun and express their creativity and personal style.

Neptune in Leo spanned the years 1587 to 1602, amplifying creative expression during the latter part of the reign of Elizabeth I. William Shakespeare's works from this period include the love story of *Romeo and Juliet* and many of his most loved comedies.

In art and architecture, the ornamental and playful Rococo style characterised the 1751–65 era, reflecting the Leo penchant for elegance, luxury and fun.

Paris in the 1920s was a hive of bohemian and artistic expression. Artists, writers and performers flocked to the city where music, art, sex and drugs were all part of an experimental culture. The city drew a host of eccentrics from across Europe, Canada and the United States. After World War I, similar bohemian centres sprang up in many cities across the globe, including Berlin, Germany and in Sydney, Australia.

The 1920s showcased the creativity of Picasso, Matisse, Cole Porter, Hemingway, Josephine Baker and Isadora Duncan, among many others. Art déco was in vogue. Despite prohibition in the United States, it too was swept up in the hedonism of the day. This was the Age of Jazz, of Broadway and the beginnings of the movie industry in Hollywood. In 1924, the Sam Goldwyn established

MGM with its iconic logo, Leo the Lion. The Sun, our star, rules Leo. With Neptune in Leo, the mythology of 'stardom' emerged. The movie industry took a major step forward with the release of *The Jazz Singer* in 1927, the first talking motion picture. The period from 1915 to 1929 saw a dynamic shift in filmmaking techniques and artistic experimentation.

People born during these years carry within them the imprint of these themes and symbols. Writers born with Neptune in Leo include: Maya Angelou, Truman Capote, Anne Frank, Alex Haley, Elizabeth Jolley and Gore Vidal.

Notable Publications

1587–1602	Numerous comedies	William Shakespeare
1759	*Candide*	Voltaire
1762	*The Social Contract*	Jean-Jacques Rousseau
1922	*Ulysses*	James Joyce
1925	*The Great Gatsby*	F. Scott Fitzgerald
1926	*The Sun Also Rises*	Ernest Hemingway
1927	*To the Lighthouse*	Virginia Woolf

Notable Films

1915	*The Birth of a Nation*
1927	*Metropolis*

Neptune in Virgo

1601–15

1764–79

1928–43

Neptune in Virgo generates a far more subdued and serious atmosphere. Virgo opposes Pisces on the zodiac wheel, so when Neptune is in Virgo, it's like a fish out of water. Consistent with this melancholy mood, between 1601 and 1615, William Shakespeare wrote many of his tragedies, including *Hamlet*, *Othello*, *King Lear* and *Macbeth*.

Neoclassicism was the main artistic and literary style during the 1764-79 period. Influenced by ancient Greek and Roman art, it is characterised by an emphasis on simplicity, rationality and morality. Written works from this era provided social commentary and an analysis of historic events, such as *The History of the Decline and Fall of the Roman Empire* (1776) by Edward Gibbon and *Evelina* (1778) by Frances Burney, a novel about a young woman attempting to navigate the expectations of society.

After the fun and frivolity of the 1920s, with Neptune again in Virgo, a more sombre tone and worried feeling emerged. The party was over and everyone, it seemed, had a collective hangover. The stock market crash of 1929 delivered a serious setback. Practical matters like the Virgo realms of work and health were centre stage as mass unemployment took hold. The collective mood was heavy and serious.

This was a difficult period which encompassed the Great Depression and World War II (see Pluto in Cancer). In Hollywood, film noir was in vogue. War films and propaganda also featured in this era. Similarly, in the 1928–43 era, trends in women's fashion became more conservative with sharper lines.

Published in 1933, Vera Brittain's memoir, *Testament of Youth*, recounts her experiences as a nurse during the WWI and its lasting impact on those who suffered significant loss. John Steinbeck wrote *Of Mice and Men* and *The Grapes of Wrath*, both of which catalogue the hardship of the Great Depression.

People born during these years carry within them the imprint of these themes and symbols. Writers born with Neptune in Virgo include: Samuel Taylor Coleridge, Germaine Greer, Erica Jong, Colleen McCullough, John Milton and Hunter S. Thompson.

Notable Publications

1605	*Don Quixote*	Miguel de Cervantes
1601–15	Numerous Tragedies	William Shakespeare
1768–71	*Encyclopedia Brittanica*	(First edition)
1932	*Brave New World*	Aldous Huxley
1933	*Testament of Youth*	Vera Brittain
1937	*Of Mice and Men*	John Steinbeck
1937	*The Hobbit*	JRR Tolkien
1939	*The Grapes of Wrath*	John Steinbeck
1940	*For Whom the Bell Tolls*	Ernest Hemingway

Notable Films

1931	*Frankenstein*
1933	*King Kong*
1934	*It Happened One Night*
1937	*Snow White and the Seven Dwarfs*
1939	*Gone with the Wind*
1939	*The Wizard of Oz*
1941	*The Maltese Falcon*
1941	*Citizen Kane*
1942	*Casablanca*

Neptune in Libra

1614–29

1778–93

1942–57

A spirit level is a device with a glass tube that contains alcohol (or other liquid) and a bubble of air. Builders use it to ensure correct alignment. Neptune in Libra operates in a similar way. It desires a level playing field and tries to correct imbalances to achieve justice. Like a spirit level, Neptune in Libra is also a combination of liquid and air.

Neptune was in Libra at the time of the storming of the Bastille in Paris in 1789. Due to economic hardship, high taxes, food shortages and social inequity, there was widespread discontent in France. People revolted, seeking to be free from poverty and their lives of disadvantage.

Cardinal air sign Libra is associated with decision-making. Neptune last entered Libra in 1942, when the world witnessed a turning point in World War II hostilities. Two major events turned the tide. Just before Neptune crossed into Libra, on 7 December 1941, the Japanese bombed the US naval base at Pearl Harbour, bringing the Americans into the war. Within days, Germany too declared war on the US. At the same time, the German advance was halted outside Moscow when the temperature plummeted to a staggering minus 40 degrees Celsius. Consistent with the union of air and water, the European winter of 1941–2 was one of the coldest on record. The Russians launched a counterattack on 5 December, which led to Hitler's first major defeat.[14] The Battle of Stalingrad

(July 1942 to February 1943) was also a major turning point. Russia successfully defended the city and launched a counteroffensive.

After the war, when the United Nations was established in 1945, Neptune, Jupiter, Chiron, Venus and Juno were all located in peaceful Libra. Venus and Neptune were exactly aligned.

Important books which discuss matters of equality, philosophy and a range of social issues have emerged when Neptune is in the sign of balance. Libra is associated with justice, so when Neptune is here, there is a widespread collective focus on social injustice and the need to address inequality.

People born during these years carry within them the imprint of these themes and symbols. Writers born with Neptune in Libra include: Lord Byron, Michael Crichton, Stephen King, Salman Rushdie, Percy Bysshe Shelley and Alice Walker.

Notable Publications

Year	Title	Author
1792	*A Vindication of the Rights of Woman*	Mary Wollstonecraft
1794	*The Age of Reason*	Thomas Paine
1781	*The Critique of Pure Reason*	Immanuel Kant
1791	*The Autobiography of Benjamin Franklin*	Benjamin Franklin
1943	*The Fountainhead*	Ayn Rand
1945	*Animal Farm*	George Orwell
1949	*Nineteen Eighty-Four*	George Orwell
1951	*The Catcher in the Rye*	JD Salinger
1953	*Fahrenheit 451*	Ray Bradbury

Notable Films

1944   *Double Indemnity*
1946   *It's a Wonderful Life*
1950   *Sunset Boulevard*
1952   *Singing in the Rain*
1953   *Roman Holiday*
1954   *Rear Window*
1954   *On the Waterfront*
1954   *Dial M for Murder*
1956   *The Ten Commandments*

Neptune in Scorpio

1628–43

1792–1807

1955–70

Neptune in Scorpio triggers a collective interest in examining the unknown, including the mysteries of life and death. This era operates similarly to Pluto in Pisces, which also joins these two archetypes together (see Pluto in Pisces). These can be profound and mysterious years and the creative output produced at these times clearly reflects this fascination.

In *Faust*, we have the tale of a man who seeks the meaning of life, but who is dissatisfied by his studies. He wants to delve deeper so he makes a pact with the devil. A battle between good and evil ensues. The tale is full of Scorpionic imagery, magic, mystery, seduction and the hope of redemption.

The most recent Neptune in Scorpio cycle (1955–70) coincided with the 1960s, deepening the process of transformation which was underway when the conjunction of Uranus and Pluto was shaking the foundations of society. Just as Neptune shifted into Scorpio, rock and roll exploded on the scene. In some circles it was labelled 'the devil's music' but it quickly gained widespread popularity, especially among the younger generation, fuelling the counterculture of the 60s.

This era produced memorable movies which explored mysterious and psychological themes, including Hitchcock's movies *Psycho*, *Vertigo* and *The Birds*. Neptune in Scorpio encourages the examination of the unknown and the depths of the human psyche. Apart from psychological thrillers and horror films, this era saw the

James Bond franchise emerge, in keeping with the Scorpio subjects of espionage and intrigue.

People born with Neptune in Scorpio are often passionate about important causes, while others seek power and control and will manipulate and deceive to advance their own interests. All are interested in the unknown and exploring hidden realms. People born during these years carry within them the imprint of these themes and symbols. Writers born with Neptune in Scorpio include: Hans Christian Andersen, Alexandre Dumas, Nathaniel Hawthorne, Victor Hugo and Mary Shelley.

Notable Publications

1632	*Dialogues on the Two Chief Systems of the World*	Mary Wollstonecraft
1808	*Faust*	Thomas Paine
1961	*Catch-22*	Immanuel Kant
1962	*One Flew Over the Cuckoo's Nest*	Benjamin Franklin
1965	*In Cold Blood*	Ayn Rand

Notable Films

1955 *Rebel Without a Cause*
1958 *Vertigo*
1960 *Psycho*
1962 *To Kill a Mockingbird*
1962 *Lawrence of Arabia*
1964 *Dr Strangelove or: How I Learned to Stop Worrying and Love the Bomb*
1968 *2001: A Space Odyssey*

1968   *Rosemary's Baby*
1969   *Easy Rider*
1969   *Midnight Cowboy*

Neptune in Sagittarius

1642–57

1806–21

1970–84

Under the influence of expansive Jupiter, Neptune in Sagittarius produced the grandeur of the Baroque period, which emerged in Europe circa 1642. Artists produced monuments, art and architecture on a grand scale. Awe-inspiring dynamic compositions featured intense religious themes, especially in Spain and Italy.

The 1806–21 transit sparked the Romantic movement with poetry by Byron, Keats and many others. Jane Austen's six novels were published between 1811 and 1817. *Northanger Abbey* and *Persuasion* were published posthumously, after her death in 1817.

Neptune in Sagittarius resonates with an abundance of spiritual and mutable vibrations. It opens a vast array of possibilities. Nothing is concrete, nothing is forever, nothing is real. Everything is in flux, everything is changing and anything is possible. As we seek spiritual meaning, eventually we might discover we are deluding ourselves, but the journey is certainly interesting.

Neptune in Sagittarius is a curious blend of the mystical and the experimental. It's fluid and expansive. We can clearly see this throughout the most recent sojourn of Neptune in Sagittarius between 1970 and 1984. The spiritual renaissance that grew out of the '60s hippie culture became known as the New Age movement. Clothing was colourful and free-flowing. Platform shoes, flares, paisley designs, kaftans and culottes were some of the over-the-top fashion trends.

Neptune and Sagittarius both foster a longing for spiritual meaning. It's no surprise that this transit inspires the human desire for faith and belief. This was the era of the cult, of Jim Jones' Jonestown, the Bhagwan's Orange people and the Hare Krishna movement. In the early 1970s, *Linda Goodman's Sun Signs* revived a mass interest in astrology. This was also the era of 'god rock', of *Jesus Christ Superstar* and *Godspell*. Even the Lord's Prayer was put to music and given commercial airplay. George Harrison released 'My Sweet Lord' on 23 November 1970. Hollywood was producing movies like *Close Encounters of the Third Kind* and *E.T.*

Those born during these years carry within them the imprint of these themes and symbols. Writers born with Neptune in Sagittarius include: Elizabeth Barrett Browning, Charles Dickens, George Eliot, Karl Marx, Herman Melville and Lord Alfred Tennyson.

Notable Publications

Year	Title	Author
1813	*Pride and Prejudice* & other work	Jane Austen
1818	*Frankenstein*	Mary Shelley
1819	*Don Juan*	Lord Byron
1968	*Linda Goodman's Sun Signs*	Linda Goodman
1972	*The Joy of Sex*	Alex Comfort
1973	*Fear of Flying*	Erica Jong
1976	*Roots*	Alex Haley
1979	*The Hitchhiker's Guide to the Galaxy*	Douglas Adams
1982	*The Color Purple*	Alice Walker

Notable Films

1971 *A Clockwork Orange*
1972 *The Godfather*
1973 *The Exorcist*
1975 *One Flew Over the Cuckoo's Nest*
1977 *Star Wars*
1977 *Close Encounters of the Third Kind*
1980 *The Shining*
1981 *Raiders of the Lost Ark*
1982 *E.T. the Extra-Terrestrial*
1982 *Blade Runner*

Neptune in Capricorn

1656–72

1820–35

1984–98

Capricorn sits at the pinnacle of the zodiac wheel. In a collective sense, the mix of the cardinal modality with the earth element manifests through governments and political systems. With Neptune here, we witness the dissolving of boundaries and systems and the formation of new borders and political alliances, as happened in Europe in the 1990s with the fall of communism.

After the magical, mystical and expansive years of Neptune in Sagittarius, Capricorn takes us down to earth, ushering in a far more serious atmosphere. Saturn governs Capricorn and it concerns itself with limitations, restrictions and responsibilities. Since Neptune is the planet we associate with the avoidance of reality, this combination can evoke a sombre mood which can leave us feeling rather depressed and disillusioned. On the positive side, it can also dissolve brutal regimes and practices, delivering more empathy and understanding.

During the 1984–98 transit of Neptune in Capricorn, long-standing traditions and systems were eroded, leading to a collective mood of uncertainty. The stock market crash of 1987 plunged the world into a global recession. There was widespread unemployment, which contributed to a loss of purpose and low self-esteem. Rapid globalisation, market-driven economics, retrenchments, downsizing and job insecurity fuelled an epidemic of depression.

In keeping with Capricorn/Saturn, fashion trends in this era were dark and austere, featuring corporate power dressing with its huge shoulder pads. Grey and black colours were everywhere.

At this time, the grunge style emerged with its torn clothing and downtrodden look, which speaks to Capricorn's austerity. Many of the books and films of this period, such as *Paradise Lost*, *The Handmaid's Tale*, and *Schindler's List*, reflect these motifs.

Those born with Neptune in Capricorn carry within them the imprint of these themes and symbols. Writers born with Neptune in Capricorn include: Louisa May Alcott, Lewis Carroll, Emily Dickinson, Anna Sewell, Leo Tolstoy and Jules Verne.

Notable Publications

1667	*Paradise Lost*	John Milton
1831	*The Hunchback of Notre-Dame*	Victor Hugo
1985	*The Handmaid's Tale*	Margaret Atwood
1988	*A Brief History of Time*	Stephen Hawking
1996	*A Game of Thrones*	George RR Martin

Notable Films

1984	*The Terminator*
1984	*Indiana Jones and the Temple of Doom*
1986	*Platoon*
1990	*Goodfellas*
1991	*The Silence of the Lambs*
1993	*Jurassic Park*
1993	*Schindler's List*
1994	*Pulp Fiction*
1994	*The Shawshank Redemption*
1995	*Braveheart*
1997	*Titanic*

Neptune in Aquarius

1671–86

1834–49

1998–2012

When astronomers discovered Neptune in 1846, it was in the sign of Aquarius. The discovery of new planets calls forth its associated themes and symbols, heralding the emergence of new paradigms and beliefs. This era stirred an interest in hypnosis, anaesthetics and spiritualism.

Neptune in Aquarius seems to possess an equal fascination for the scientific and the spiritual. True to the disparate elements of water and air, Neptune and Aquarius have very different perspectives. Communication between air and water is difficult at the best of times. Potentially, Neptune in Aquarius offers us an opportunity to combine the scientific ideas and technology of Aquarius with the spiritual understanding and empathy of Neptune, creating a holistic and compassionate worldview. However, the intrinsic differences between air and water make this difficult to attain. As a result, Neptune in Aquarius can polarise opinions, such as far left and far right extremism. Religion versus science is another example of the split which can manifest in this cycle.

Towards the end of the zodiac, the realm of collective concepts and universal themes is amplified. Neptune rules the oceans and the weather. Cyclones, tornados, tsunamis, severe storms, floods and earthquakes are all the domain of Neptune. With its natural affinity with Aquarius, Uranus is known for its extreme and unpredictable character. Indeed, the Boxing Day earthquake and tsunami in 2004 and the Fukushima quake and tsunami in 2011 took place when

Neptune was in Aquarius.[15] During the recent transit of Neptune in Aquarius, there was a deluge of disaster films, featuring a host of apocalyptic catastrophes and end of the world scenarios.[16]

Those born during these years carry within them the imprint of these themes and symbols. Writers born with Neptune in Aquarius include: Thomas Hardy, Henry James, William James, William Morris, Friedrich Nietzsche and Mark Twain.

Notable Publications

1516	*Utopia*	Thomas More
1834	*The Last Days of Pompeii*	Edward Bulwer-Lytton
1838	*Oliver Twist*	Charles Dickens
1844	*The Count of Monte Cristo*	Alexandre Dumas
1845	*The Raven*	Edgar Allan Poe
1847	*Wuthering Heights*	Emily Brontë
1848	*The Communist Manifesto*	Karl Marx and Friedrich Engels

Notable Films

1998 *Armageddon*
1998 *Deep Impact*
1999 *The Matrix*
1999 *The Sixth Sense*
2000 *The Perfect Storm*
2004 *The Day after Tomorrow*
2009 *Avatar*
2009 *2012*
2011 *Melancholia*
2012 *The Impossible*

Neptune in Pisces

1685–99

1848–63

2011–25

Since its discovery in 1846, astrologers have seen the gradual erosion of Jupiter's ancient rulership of Pisces. Modern astrologers were quick to accept the lord of the oceans as the ruling planet of the sign of the fishes. It's a good fit. Neptune's natural affinity with Pisces amplifies its resonance. This is a fluid atmosphere of mystical images and dreams, overflowing with spiritual and universal concepts. When it's immersed in its own sign, Neptune seeks peace, harmony and redemption from the harsh realities of life. There is also a tendency towards escapism and the avoidance of reality.

One interesting manifestation of Neptune in Pisces took place in 1691–2 with the Salem witch hunts. Mass hysteria took hold of the population, probably spurred on by the puritanical religious beliefs within the community. Rye ergot, a type of mould which grows on rye, might have been responsible for the hysterical outpourings and hallucinations. Ergot fungus is a known hallucinogen and the effects of ergot poisoning include paranoia, muscle twitching and spasms. A cold winter followed by a wet spring creates the perfect conditions for the fungus to thrive. Hallucinations, dampness, witchcraft, mass hysteria and poisoning are all themes symptomatic of mysterious Neptune and Pisces.

When Neptune is in its own sign, it can amplify hysterical delusions. We all possess a personal unconscious that swims within the collective unconscious. The unconscious mind facilitates hypnosis, faith healing and other psychic phenomena, such as the placebo effect. Belief and suggestion operate subtly, but powerfully. In 1858, Marie Bernadette Soubirous claimed to have seen visions of the Virgin Mary at Lourdes, a miraculous story which continues to inspire Catholic pilgrims to this day. During this era, books featuring water, such as *Moby-Dick,* captured the imagination.

With Neptune recently in Pisces, we've been immersed in global oil and water issues and witnessed the gradual but continual rise in sea levels. This era saw the rapid expansion of streaming services like Netflix with a host of new players entering the market. While we have been watching movies, exploring virtual reality and engaging in social media distractions, plastic has been filling our oceans, climate change has escalated and water has emerged as the most important of all natural resources.

Those born during these years carry within them the imprint of these themes and symbols. Writers born with Neptune in Pisces include: Sir Arthur Conan Doyle, Edith Nesbit, Alexander Pope, George Bernard Shaw, Robert Louis Stevenson and Oscar Wilde.

Notable Publications

1687	*Principia Mathematica*	Isaac Newton
1851	*Moby-Dick*	Herman Melville
1852	*Uncle Tom's Cabin*	Harriet Beecher Stowe
1852	*Roget's Thesaurus*	Peter Mark Roget
1859	*On the Origin of Species*	Charles Darwin

Notable Films

2013	*Gravity*
2013	*12 Years a Slave*
2014	*The Grand Budapest Hotel*

2016 *La La Land*
2019 *Parasite*
2019 *Once Upon a Time in Hollywood*
2020 *Nomadland*
2021 *Don't Look Up*
2022 *Everything Everywhere All at Once*
2022 *Avatar: The Way of Water*
2023 *Barbie*

5. BRINGING IT ALL TOGETHER

Stellar Word Selection

Many words come to us from the language of astrology. Some words have obvious links to the planets and astrological concepts, but some words have astrological origins that are not so obvious. Words like 'disaster', for example, which means disconnected or separated from the stars. The inference here is similar to the proverb 'pride goes before a fall'. If we think we are separate from the universe, or ignorant of the interconnections between all living things, then this attitude invites accidents and disasters.

Learning more about etymology and the origin of words can reveal some interesting facts. I've included a list of words that have astrological origins or associations. Before you decide to use any of these terms, make sure you investigate the source of these words, so you fully understand their true meaning and symbolism. For example, if you are writing a romance novel, or indeed any story where you want to focus on a romantic moment, you can include a host of words and concepts associated with Venus, the planet of love.

'It was a Friday in April when I came across the shiny copper pot in the plant nursery. The flowers were in full bloom, their beautiful petals opening just for me. It was at that moment I knew how much I really loved him.'

Word	Origin or Interpretation
Amalgam	Mercury.
Amalgamate	Mercury.
Annual	Yearly.
Aphrodisiac	Inducing sexual desire. Venus (Aphrodite).
Aphrodite	Greek counterpart of Venus.
April	Month named for Aphrodite (Venus).
Aquarius	11th sign of the zodiac.
Archer	Symbol for Sagittarius.
Aries	1st sign of the zodiac.
Ascendant	The zodiac sign rising in the east.
Ascendancy	Rising.
Ascending	Rising.
Aspect	To observe.
Asterisk	Little star.
Asteroid	Like a small star.
Astronomical	Immense, like a star.
Athena	Asteroid goddess of wisdom.
Athens	City named for Athena.
Bull	Symbol for Taurus.
Cancer	4th sign of the zodiac.
Capricious	Sudden movement. Like a wild goat, apt to jump about.
Capricorn	10th sign of the zodiac.
Centaur	Symbol for Sagittarius and Chiron.
Cereal	Ceres.
Ceres	Asteroid goddess of crops and nature.
Chiromancy	Palmistry. Chiron.
Chiron	Chiro, the hand. Chiron.

Word	Origin or Interpretation
Chiropody	Healing of the feet using the hands. Chiron.
Chiropractor	Healing manipulation using the hands. Chiron.
Chronic	Condition of long standing. Saturn/Cronus.
Chronicle	Saturn/Cronus.
Chronology	Saturn/Cronus.
Commerce	Mercury.
Conjunction	Two or more planets together.
Consider	To observe the stars. See Sidereal.
Considerable	To observe the stars. See Sidereal.
Considerate	To observe the stars. See Sidereal.
Consideration	To observe the stars. See Sidereal.
Constellation	A collection of stars or planets.
Copper	Alchemical metal of Venus.
Crab	Symbol for Cancer.
Crescendo	Gradual increase. Crescent Moon.
Crescent	Crescent Moon.
Desire	To await what the stars will bring. See Sidereal.
Disaster	Separated from the stars.
Eclipse	Failing to appear.
Ecliptic	The path of the Sun and planets.
Elementary	Fundamental. Of the elements.
Equinox	The Sun crossing the equator. Equal day and night.
February	Month of purification.
Fishes	Symbol for Pisces.
Focus	Hearth/fireplace. See Vesta.
Friday	Day of the week named for Frigga/Venus.
Gemini	3rd sign of the zodiac.

Word	Origin or Interpretation
Goat	Symbol for Capricorn.
Gold	Alchemical metal of the Sun.
Honeymoon	The sweet month after the wedding. Moon.
Horoscope	To observe the hour (of birth).
Hygiea	Asteroid goddess of healing.
Hygiene	Hygiea.
Inconsiderate	Thoughtless. Not observing the stars. See Sidereal.
Influence	An emanation from the stars.
Influential	See Influence.
Influenza	An illness emanating from the stars. See Influence.
Iron	Alchemical metal of Mars.
January	Month named for the Roman god Janus.
Jove	Jupiter.
Jovial	Jupiter.
June	Month named for Juno.
Juno	Asteroid goddess of marriage.
Jupiter	The largest planet in our solar system.
Lead	Alchemical metal of Saturn.
Leo	5th sign of the zodiac.
LB (Libra Pondo)	Measure of weight. Libra.
Libra	7th sign of the zodiac.
Lion	Symbol for Leo.
Lucifer	Bringer of light. Venus as the morning star.
Lunar	Moon.
Lunatic	Influenced by the Moon.
Many happy… returns	When the Sun returns to its birth position. See Return.
March	Month named for Mars.

Word	Origin or Interpretation
Market(ing)	Mercury.
Mars	Roman god of war.
Martial	Mars.
May	Month named for Roman goddess Maia.
Meniscus	Crescent Moon shaped.
Menopause	Moon.
Menstrual	Moon.
Menstruation	Moon.
Mercantile	Mercury.
Mercenary	One who does anything for money. Mercury.
Merchandise	Mercury.
Merchant	Mercury.
Mercurial	Changeable. Mercury.
Mercury	Alchemical metal of Mercury.
Mercy	Mercury.
Monday	Day of the week named for the Moon.
Month	Moon.
Moonshine	Moon.
Mother	Moon.
Neptunium	Element named after Neptune.
Opposition	Planets aligned on opposite sides of the Earth.
Phase	A particular stage in a process of development. Moon.
Pisces	12th sign of the zodiac.
Pluto	Pluto.
Plutonium	Metallic element named after Pluto.
Pound weight	Libra (LB).
Quicksilver	Mercury.

Word	Origin or Interpretation
Ram	Symbol for Aries.
Reconsider	See Sidereal.
Return	To return to its former position. (Sun, Moon and planets).
Reverence	See Venerate. Venus.
Revolution	Orbital revolution of a planet that can herald upheaval.
Revolve	To orbit around a central point.
Sagittarius	9th sign of the zodiac.
Saturday	Day of the week named for Saturn.
Saturn	Saturn the ringed planet.
Saturnalia	Roman festival honouring Saturn.
Saturnian	Like Saturn.
Saturnine	Sluggish, gloomy, cold.
Scales	Symbol for Libra.
Scorpio	8th sign of the zodiac.
Scorpion	Symbol for Scorpio.
Selenite	Moonstone.
Semester	Six months. Moon.
Sidereal	Of the stars.
Silver	Alchemical metal of the Moon.
Solar	Sol the Sun.
Solarium	Sun.
Solstice	Sun stands still at peak declination, north or south.
Sun	Sol. Our star.
Sunday	Day of the week named for the Sun.
Sunny	Sun.
Taurus	2nd sign of the zodiac.
Thermometer	Liquid Mercury in a glass tube.

Word	Origin or Interpretation
Thursday	Day of the week named for Thor/Jupiter.
Tin	Alchemical metal of Jupiter.
Trimester	Three months. Moon.
Tuesday	Day of the week named for Mars.
Twins	Symbol for Gemini.
Uranium	Rare metallic element named for Uranus.
Uranus	Uranus.
Venal/vend	Can be obtained for a price. Venus.
Venerable	Worthy of respect. Venus.
Venerate	To adore. Venus.
Venereal	Sexual desire or intercourse. Venus.
Venus	Planet of love and beauty.
Vesper	Venus as the evening star.
Vesta	Asteroid goddess of the hearth or fireplace.
Virgin	Symbol for Virgo. Unmarried.
Virgo	6th sign of the zodiac.
Water-bearer	Symbol for Aquarius.
Water-goat	Symbol for Capricorn.
Wednesday	Day of the week named for Woden/Mercury.
Zodiac	Circle of animals.

Cycles and Timelines

As we have seen, planetary cycles correspond with major life events and key decisions. The planetary cycles listed here take place at the same time of life for everyone. The squares, oppositions and returns trigger personal growth. It's the same with storytelling. What age is your main character? As the passage of time unfolds, consider what your protagonist will be experiencing at their time of life. This timetable of major life events highlights which planet underscores the tests and challenges they will encounter. As you develop your narrative, look at the symbols associated with each planet to incorporate these themes into your story.

Timetable of Major Life Events

Age[17] in years	Major Aspect
7	First Saturn square
12	First Jupiter return
14	First Saturn opposition
21	Third Saturn square
21	First Uranus square
24	Second Jupiter return
29	First Saturn return
35	Another Saturn square
36	Third Jupiter return
41	Neptune square
42	Second Saturn opposition
42	Uranus opposition
48	Fourth Jupiter return
49	Another Saturn square
51	Chiron return
56	Another Saturn square
58	Second Saturn return
60	Fifth Jupiter return
63	Second Uranus square
65	Another Saturn square
72	Third Saturn opposition
72	Sixth Jupiter return
79	Another Saturn square
84	Uranus return
84	Seventh Jupiter return
87	Third Saturn return

Story Planning Guide

You can use the following guide to plan your story, develop your main character's personality and map their journey. You might just have an idea for a particular conflict, a type of character, a certain setting, or a particular era, so start wherever you wish. Allow ideas to come to you as you develop your narrative. This is not a test, so don't feel you have to answer all these questions. These are simply suggestions for you to consider.

Your Setting

1. What time period is your story set?
2. Where are the outer planets Pluto and Neptune located?
3. How have generational influences, global events, symbols and themes fostered your protagonist's beliefs and worldview?

Your Main Character and Their Motivation

1. Is your protagonist male, female, non-binary or perhaps not human?
2. Are they an introvert or an extrovert?
3. Which astrological element best describes them?
4. Which of the three qualities best describes them?
5. Which zodiac sign, or signs, best describes them?
6. Which element do they lack?
7. Which quality do they lack?
8. How does their persona/ascendant differ from their real character?

9. What do they value most?
10. Imagine you are your main protagonist and write a brief autobiography.

Your Protagonist's Journey

1. What age is your main character?
2. How many years do you explore in your story?
3. Which planetary cycle, or cycles, will they experience?
4. Why are they undertaking this journey, what motivates them? Do they have an objective? If so, what?
5. Is there a lesson they need to learn? If so, what?

Conflict and Story Arc

1. What specific challenges will your protagonist face?
2. Which astrological archetype/s best describes their shadow/antagonist?
3. Write a brief biography of your chief antagonist.
4. Is your story a cardinal conflict, a fixed feud, or a mutable misunderstanding?
5. Which other characters will be involved? Helpers, mentors, shapeshifters, threshold guardians. Describe their character and motivation too.
6. Use a map of the hero's or heroine's journey to plan your story.
7. Write a brief story outline.

Conclusion

1. Is there a moral to the tale?
2. How is your main character changed by events?

Form

1. Who is your audience?
2. What is the genre? Is it a comedy, satire, drama, sci-fi, romance, historical fiction, horror, crime, a whodunnit?
3. Would it be better to write your story in the third person, or first person?

6. BIBLIOGRAPHY

Online material

https://www.theoi.com/ A great online encyclopedia of classical mythology.

https://www.etymonline.com/ A wonderful reference guide for word origins and meanings.

https://www.medievalastrologyguide.com/ A useful resource covering many aspects of the foundations of astrology.

https://fashionhistory.fitnyc.edu/1890-1899/

Books

Christopher Vogler, *The Writer's Journey*, Michael Wiese Productions, Studio City, CA, USA. Third Edition 2007.

Liz Greene, *Relating*, Samuel Weiser, Inc., Maine, USA, 1978.

Isabel Briggs Myers with Peter B. Myers, *Gifts Differing*, CPP, Inc., Mountain View, CA, 1980.

Dorian Gieseler Greenbaum, *Temperament, Astrology's Forgotten Key*, The Wessex Astrologer, Bournemouth, England, 2005.

Michele Finey, *Secrets of the Zodiac*, Allen and Unwin, Crows Nest, Australia, 2009, Second Imprint 2010.

Michele Finey, *The Sacred Dance of Venus and Mars*, The Wessex Astrologer, Swanage, UK, 2012, Revised Edition 2022.

7. ENDNOTES

1. https://en.wikipedia.org/wiki/Hero%27s_journey#/media/File:Heroesjourney.svg
2. Apparent retrograde motion is when planets appear to move backwards through the zodiac as viewed from Earth.
3. Original diagram first published in *The Sacred Dance of Venus and Mars* 2012.
4. The exact orbit of Jupiter is 11.862 years.
5. See also Uranus.
6. The opposite point in the Zodiac is 0 degrees of Libra which is when the Sun enters Libra each year and crosses the Equator once more, heading south. These points are determined by the tilt of the Earth and our orbital journey around the Sun.
7. https://www.washingtonpost.com/outlook/2019/07/17/true-story-behind-lion-king
8. https://www.youtube.com/watch?v=DnFeMhtQg54 Accessed September 2022.
9. https://en.wikipedia.org/wiki/John_Grisham#cite_note-Biography-9 Accessed September 2022.

10. https://www.nationalgeographic.com/animals/invertebrates/facts/scorpions Accessed September 2022.

11. https://www.etymonline.com/search?q=february Accessed January 2023.

12. The semi-square and the sesquisquare are important aspects but are not listed in this table.

13. Uranus was also in Gemini by this time. Gutenberg was born circa 1399.

14. https://hal.science/hal-01379274/document Will Slauter. The Rise of the Newspaper. Richard R. John and Jonathan Silberstein-Loeb. Making News: The Political Economy of Journalism in Britain and America from the Glorious Revolution to the Internet, 2015, 9780199676187. ffhal-01379274f. Accessed June 2023.

15. https://en.wikipedia.org/wiki/The_Spectator_(1711) Accessed May 2025.

16. These turning points took place with Neptune located at 29.40 of Virgo. Neptune did not move into Libra until October 1942, but continued to hover around the last degree of Virgo for over a year before crossing into Libra. The last degree of any sign foreshadows imminent change.

17. At the time of both disasters, Uranus was in Pisces, creating an additional symbolic link between these archetypes.

18. *Titanic* was released in 1997, just prior to this transit.

19. Allow an orb of up to one year to allow for retrograde motion.

www.ingramcontent.com/pod-product-compliance
Lightning Source LLC
Chambersburg PA
CBHW061216070526
44584CB00029B/3855